The Gardens
of
San Francisco

A 1915 view of San Francisco, showing the undeveloped hills and the site of the Exposition along the northern waterfront. (Courtesy University of California, Berkeley, Map collection)

The Gardens
of
San Francisco

by

JOAN HOCKADAY

with photographs
by

HENRY BOWLES

TIMBER PRESS
Portland, Oregon

ISBN 0-88192-104-1
Printed in Singapore

Timber Press
9999 SW Wilshire
Portland, Oregon 97225

Library of Congress Cataloging-in-Publication Data

Hockaday, Joan.
    The gardens of San Francisco / by Joan Hockaday ; with photographs
by Henry Bowles.
        p.   cm.
    Includes index.
    ISBN 0-88192-104-1
    1. Gardens--California--San Francisco. 2. Gardens--California-
-San Francisco--Pictorial works. 3. San Francisco (Calif.)-
-Description.   I. Bowles, Henry.   II. Title.
SB466.U65H63 1988
712'.5'09794--dc19   88-19767
                                                                   CIP

CONTENTS

DEDICATION

This book is dedicated to four San Franciscans who have shaped this book as much as did the architects of the City Beautiful Movement a century ago.

To Dorothy Erskine, the champion of San Francisco's open spaces and hill-tops, whose cheery call to action was familiar to all who cherish this city's beauty.

To her sister, Jean Wolff, a most patient gardening teacher, who inspired a generation of San Franciscans in the art of pleasure gardening. She was the first to share her enthusiasm, and wisdom, for *The Gardens of San Francisco* at its inception three years ago.

To Ted Kipping, a most able tree surgeon, who climbed down from the treetops just long enough to share the beauty he had seen from his vantage point above the finest San Francisco gardens.

To Henry Bowles, who translated this beauty into the handsome private garden photographs seen on the following pages.

Lupine and other native flowers bloom all spring above Baker Beach on the fragile sand hills.

I. THE SEASONS

When the rest of the country turns to Spring, Summer, Autumn and Winter, gardeners envision frost nipping pretty new buds, heat wilting colorful flowers, color lighting the countryside, and snow smothering burlap-covered bushes. San Franciscans have none of these images close to home. The freezing temperatures, the heat, the humidity, the blaze of color, and the freshly fallen snow, are invigorating yet non-existent, or only occasional visitors, in this seaside city.

The seasons unfold subtly in San Francisco, with spring wildflowers lighting the hills, with summer fog horns brooding by the Golden Gate, with the arrival, finally, of warm, windless, sunny days in autumn, with the sound of the first raindrops, signaling the wet winter to come.

The fog is the bellwether, is the reason San Franciscans need not look up from their tasks to know that the wind is coming, or the mist is about to envelop. The fog keeps the plants moist during the rainless summers, while, only 15 miles away, summer sun withers plants in place. Aptly named morsels—'Frisco Fogger' tomatoes, for instance—are snatched up despite a bland flavor; the romance is in the name, and the nurserymen know it.

Gardens and parks in San Francisco have special requirements, well met by an enthusiastic citizenery spoiled by natural beauty, and intent upon adding to it at every turn. The parks are among the best-kept in the country, and the gardens are almost without equal for tiny town enclosures. The seasons fooled the early settlers, challenged their successors and contribute to the uniqueness of the plants in the parks and gardens sprinkled everywhere, hidden or exposed to view.

Pollarded trees in Golden Gate Park Music Concourse. The sunken garden takes on a more formal aspect in winter when the bare trees show their shape and allow sunlight through.

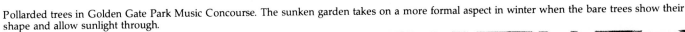

Spring arrives in February well before the famous groundhog finds out whether winter will end in Punxsutawney, Pennsylvania, 2,000 miles away. The yellow of the acacia, the pink of the plum and the many colors of camellia blossoms come as early as January, in warmer pockets, followed by wisteria and traditional spring bulbs. Each season arrives a month ahead of its counterpart in the Pacific Northwest, and a good two months before the same season on the northeast Atlantic coast. San Francisco seasons even defy Bay Area calendars and clocks; city gardens come into bloom a little later, a week or 10 days, than those in the surrounding countryside.

On the lower Greenwich Street Steps, below Montgomery, flowering trees and bulbs make a fine spring display in February.

A Telegraph Hill stairway bursts into bloom in mid-February.

Along these Forest Hill Steps, a doctor tends this garden and keeps a constant supply of flowers growing for commuters to pick on their way to work.

Some roses continue blooming into the San Francisco summer, although most put on their best show in April and May. The seasons unfold early in the maritime climate of San Francisco.

The summer, however, sets San Francisco apart perhaps more than any other season. The wind announces the oncoming fog, and summer visitors huddle in their flimsy Hawaiian shirts against these forces coming in from the sea. As temperatures rise inland, baking the gardens of the interior, the offshore fog is drawn in through the Golden Gate to cool off the coast and blanket the flowers—those special flowers that will bloom in the fog. Hawaii is miles away, with little in common except for its Pacific Ocean address.

San Francisco writer Harold Gilliam, years ago, unwrapped the mystery of the fog and its phenomenon in a tiny pamphlet entitled *Weather*. The fog, he tells us, is quite different in winter and summer, and he tells us why. Most city gardeners own a copy of *Weather*, if for no other reason than to explain the beauty of the fog to inquiring visitors.

The fog in summer is wind-blown and white rather than stagnant and murky; it is light and often causes an admirer to squint in the brightness. When the heat waves come in summer—that is, when the temperature rises above 80°F—San Franciscans open their windows and wait for the natural air-conditioning to rescue them from the heat spell. Rarely does the heat last more than two days—on the third day, almost without fail, the fog rolls in on its way toward the warm interior.

The clear bright light sharpens or softens the color of the flowers, depending on the season and the

The Russian Hill hydrangeas on the Crookedest Street in The World (which was a straight steep incline until the 1920s) attract thousands of tourists in summer, although Peter Bercut planted the flowers simply to beautify his street. Best seen from Hyde Street Cable Car, which passes directly above the Lombard Street garden.

intended result. In the midst of the fog which rushes in through the gap in the Golden Gate, the vivid, pretty Golden Gate Bridge garden, by the south tower, is testament to the flower variety and color possible under a bright but soggy blanket. A mile or two south, in Golden Gate Park, with its century-old windbreak in place, the flowers take on an even brighter hue, although the meadows are the first to feel freezing temperatures on rare occasions when the thermometer dips below 32° in winter.

Autumn arrives with the Naked Lady (*Amaryllis belladonna*) blooming on the hillside beneath the Golden Gate Bridge and in larger, old-fashioned gardens all over the city. The dahlia garden in Golden Gate Park reaches its peak after the summer tourists leave, and the trees begin a slow, subtle change in color which lasts well into December in warmer sections of the city. The gradual unfolding of the seasons, autumn particularly, is again in contrast to the dramatic, overnight transformation of vegetation in colder climates.

Winter brings almost 25 inches of needed rain to the city, while outlying areas receive almost twice as much. Between rain storms, the clear, warm, winter days are excellent for planting. Pioneer plantsman Adolph Sutro was the first to preach the merits of December planting: the roots get off to a good start while abundant rainwater soaks the ground all season. Berries, bougainvillea and citrus brighten the city at holiday time, as the gardening year comes to an end by San Francisco Bay.

Fuchsias drape over the Filbert Street Steps all summer. The Bay Bridge and East Bay are in distant view.

Vivid flower colors emerge under the bright fog cover of San Francisco summer. Flowers last longer protected from intense heat; here, *Cistus* 'Doris Hibberson' makes its pretty early summer display at the Golden Gate Bridge Garden.

When the pink *Amaryllis belladonna* nod their tall flowers in late August or early September, summer officially ends in San Francisco. These hardy old-fashioned bulbs come back year after year at Fort Point beneath the Golden Gate Bridge. City skyline in distance.

Ginkgo trees in Chinatown park, across the street from the Cable Car Barn. The Ginkgo is a symbolic tree in the Orient and makes a fine fall display, often lasting through December, in the shelter of Chinatown.

In Sydney Walton Square, normally packed with downtown office workers seeking sun and sward, trees turn color, slowly, in autumn.

Autumn leaves linger on the trees surrounding the Palace of Fine Arts, a remnant from the 1915 Panama Pacific Exposition. The Marina District surrounds the relic and occupies the entire site of the fair.

Cotoneaster lacteus (C. parneyi) berries at the Golden Gate Bridge Garden in January. Berries in abundance last well into winter in the mild San Francisco climate.

Berry and flower together on low-growing *Cotoneaster horizontalis* carpeting Lone Mountain hillside in December.

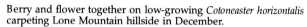

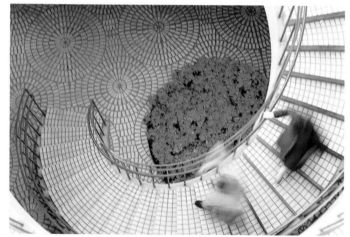

Downtown highrise owners vie with one another for the best Christmas display. At Embarcadero Center, even the darkest recess, below grade, is brightened by poinsettia show in December.

Storm clouds roll past the National Cemetery above the Presidio and Golden Gate Bridge, left. Strawberry and other tenacious native plants take hold in the cemetery during winter rains.

II. THE EARLY DAYS

San Francisco, as any city, owes its design integrity first, to geological forces, and then to men with or without vision. John McLaren and Adolph Sutro shaped the western shore, sailors and quarrymen sculptured the eastern shore, and nature, until quite recently, dominated the hills and southwest lakes. The northern shoreline, the stretch of waterfront captured on postcard, in song and in poem, owes its beauty to the permanent presence of a mighty force: the military and its fortifications, grandly guarding the Golden Gate.

The Military Guards the Gate

The crumbling cliffs of Fort Miley, the stretch of sand on the Presidio's western shore beneath the exposed bluffs by the Golden Gate Bridge, the beacon and battlements of Ft. Point, the curved, filled, military marshlands, and the remnants of officers' old-fashioned gardens spilling down the Fort Mason hillside, all, without plan, define San Francisco's past and determine its future. The islands in the bay fortified the city, too; the Army early on claimed the "Rock"—Alcatraz—long before prisoners reluctantly set up quarters in cellblocks where once pretty gardens and even a tennis court stood.

If, today, a military posting to the fortifications beside the Golden Gate seems an ideal assignment, it has not always been so. The dreary early landscape, void of vegetation and buffeted by winds year-round (but especially in summer), made a San Francisco assignment one to be dreaded.

When the Spanish claimed the land in 1776, a fort, of necessity, went up by the Golden Gate. The mission, however, housing padres and peaceful Indians, occupied a sheltered site three miles south, near a lake called La Laguna de Nuestra Senora de Los Dolores. Days before the Declaration of Independence was signed, this sleepy mission established the Spanish presence on a peninsula protecting a fine natural bay. The Presidio and Mission survived through the period of Mexican rule which followed, in the early 1800s, before the Americans established their presence in 1846.

The Presidio hills, in those pioneering years, were sprinkled with wildflowers in spring and graceful brown grasses in fall. The few native oak trees provided minimum shelter against the harsh winds; and these were mostly felled for firewood. Willow trees lined the creeks and natural fresh water supply, but the northern tip of the peninsula held few, if any, Redwood (*Sequoia sempervirens*) trees, so abundant on the coastline to the north and south of the city. The sand dunes and the redwoods were ill-suited to one another, and the rainfall, so essential to the redwood's survival, is only half that of surrounding coastal hills supporting redwood groves.

Gardens soon flourished, not only on the mainland, but on the U.S. Army post in the middle of San Francisco Bay. In the gardens on Alcatraz—a 22-acre "Rock", aptly named—only the toughest vegetation survived until soil from the mainland came, barged in from the Presidio. The bountiful garden, pictured here, shows a post-Civil-War success on Alcatraz Island.

Meanwhile, the Presidio itself—1400 acres in all, larger than Golden Gate Park—was as forlorn as when the Spanish settled here a century earlier. Not until 1882, when the commander of the post, Major General Irwin McDowell, ordered a massive tree-planting, did the present evergreen landscape begin to take its form. And not soon enough for the lonely outpost. The recruits, for years, complained about dust and sand blowing through their parlors, until finally, all the houses were moved on end so that the sand could enter through the back—kitchen—door. In addition, a 15-ft. high baffle, made of white-painted lattice, lined the walkways and anchored ivy and other climbing plants that soon smothered the windbreak.

These early efforts to hold back the wind soon gave way to the ambitious tree-planting plan of Major General McDowell's. Appropriately long of title—"Plan for the Cultivation of Trees Upon the Presidio Reservation"—the plan took a decade to carry through. With the help of schoolchildren on Arbor Day, the help of Adolph Sutro (who donated hundreds of seedlings), and help from Golden Gate Park nursery supplies (Major General McDowell also served on the city park commission), the extensive tree planting provides the framework seen today from surrounding properties.

As planned, the Presidio ridges were planted with trees, to accentuate the height of the hills; the valleys were kept clear and sunny. Dozens of different species took hold, but the strong survived—Monterey Pine, Monterey Cypress and Blue Gum—and continue to seed themselves a century later. Deciduous trees were excluded; their thin leaves and intolerance to wind scotched their place in pioneering the windy peninsula, although today, with wind protection in place, deciduous trees survive with the hardiest evergreens.

With a background of deep green dotted with blues and reds of eucalyptus leaves and flowers, the valley and its fort took on a dramatic presence which stands today as a monument to foresight and precision planning. Avenues of palms, which cast less shadow than pines and cypresses, line the valley floor, and recall the era where palms, in formal rows, were fashionable. The pioneers, the soldiers, cared not what was in fashion, but rather, what kept the sand from the back door.

Major General McDowell, his engineer, W. A. Jones, Adolph Sutro and the park nurserymen, left a legacy that today appears to be crumbling in places, but a new 40-year plan to revitalize the decaying vegetation is now in place. Within a decade, the regeneration of the military base planting will be evident and a new generation of San Franciscans will wonder at the dense 'forest' in their midst, a manufactured 'forest' designed to rim the city's north shore with evergreens. The old Presidio trees, within the next decade, must be thinned, shaped or felled to guarantee the survival of seedlings in the ambitious windbreak and beautification program begun a century ago. Only this time, the trees will be phased in, rather than planted all at once, as a century ago.

Fort Point, at the turn of the century. The lightkeeper kept his garden beside the sheltered house below the cliff, on the site of a grassed-over picnic area today. The Golden Gate Bridge now links Fort Point to the Marin shore in the distance. (Courtesy Ft. Point and Army Museum Association, San Francisco)

The Presidio was a lonely outpost in 1816, when the Spanish occupied the peninsula. Oak trees scattered in sheltered ravines served as fuel for early settlers; few other trees existed on the windy site.
(Courtesy Milton B. Halsey, Jr., Fort Point and Army Museum Association)

Mission Dolores, settled in 1776, sited inland from the windswept Presidio. A courtyard encloses a small garden surrounding gravesites of pioneers on the peninsula. (Courtesy Fort Point and Army Museum Association)

As late as 1880, the Presidio was a treeless and forlorn military outpost, until an Army commander ordered massive tree planting on the fort. This young mother wheels her baby buggy past early planting designed to hold the shifting sands. (Courtesy Fort Point and Army Museum Association)

Pine trees, recently planted on the Presidio reservation, 1882. (Courtesy Fort Point and Army Museum Association)

A tall lattice windbreak, planted in climbing vines and flowers, kept the shifting sand from the officers' doorways, and provided promenade for woman and children to stroll in this 1905 view. (Courtesy Fort Point and Army Museum Association)

Rows of cannon balls surround the tennis court and grass lawn on the windswept 'Rock'—Alcatraz—in this 19th Century view, when the Army settled this island in San Francisco Bay.
(Courtesy National Maritime Museum, San Francisco)

Flowers and fruits fill this garden on Alcatraz Island, shown in the 1880s. Military personnel admire their handiwork while the tennis court is idle, beyond the neatly stacked cannon balls. The hills of San Francisco are just barely visible, beyond. (Courtesy Bancroft Library, University of California, Berkeley)

A curious gardening custom, decidedly military, took hold early on Alcatraz, then found its way to the mainland fort. As if to signal mighty strength, with, unfortunately, only the seagulls paying attention, huge cannon balls, weighing 440 pounds each, encircled the salad beds and bordered tennis courts and roadways. Hauled off for scrap during the last world war, the 15-inch garden adornments added a dimension to older military gardens that could hardly be matched in civilian quarters. Smaller cannon balls today line the Presidio Museum entrance.

The gardens of Fort Mason (the Spanish called it Punta Medanos, or Point Sand Dunes), two miles east of the Presidio and the Golden Gate, are a bit more sheltered from the prevailing westerlies, so the lee side of the hill offers better gardening. Establishing its ownership was, however, a bitter land battle, fought in the quiet halls of Congress, 3,000 miles away. Neglected by both military and civilian settlers, the fort regained its stature after the gold strike and during the Civil War. In the 1850s, prominent citizens put up large houses and enclosed green gardens on the lee side of the fort, then called Point San Jose. The military moved in during the 1860s, evicting these "squatters", then turned the fine homes into "officers' housing".

One of the officers, however, was the same commander who, five years later, laid the groundwork for the Presidio tree planting: Major General Irwin McDowell. His home was at Point San Jose, and he determined, first, to beautify this small point of land. The native laurel grove gave the point a natural beauty; the deep green color offering a strong contrast to the white sand hills. Soon San Franciscans dubbed it "Black Point," for its vegetation, while Maj. Gen. McDowell enhanced the remainder of the post.

He ordered lupine and barley planted, then put up wooden fences to hold back the sand at a time when Golden Gate Park dune restoration was in its infancy. By the end of the 1870s, Point San Jose was all spruced up for the visit of General U.S. Grant, and, a year later, for President and Mrs. Hayes' visit. Maj. Gen. McDowell's own residence, on the lee side of the fort, was of course well manicured and void of shifting sand and other annoyances.

San Franciscans had little need or want to visit this isolated fort—the blowing sand between the fort and the city kept away all but the most curious. The officers inherited a remote, picturesque point of land but the ousted citizens succeeded, at any rate, in reducing the overall size of Fort Mason, which today remains an isolated point of land—an island of green surrounded by apartments, supermarkets and tourist attractions.

Living so near the sea had its advantages along with the isolation. The lighthouse keeper's garden at Ft. Point (remnants are visible still behind the fort) provided an abundance of flowers for children to sell, at 15 cents a bunch, to visitors who found their way to this northern-most point of San Francisco. During the glamourous 1915 Panama Pacific Exposition, which stretched along the shore between the lonely Ft. Point Lighthouse and the newly spiffed-up Fort Mason, visitors came from around the world to view the elaborate architecture—and to marvel at the flowers which grew so well out of doors, in the windy lighthouse garden. "The people from the East would go into ecstacies over them (the flowers), especially Shasta daisies and geraniums," recalls the lightkeeper's granddaughter, Merian Nagel.

The open fields around the Presidio and Fort Point supported dozens of native flowers, in addition to the ever-present poppy. After the marshland was filled in for the 1915 Fair, the remote post—and the stunning fields of flowers—became even more accessible to the 'city' dwellers, two miles away.

"When the flag lilies (wild iris) were in bloom, flower vendors would come out from the city and pull up the lilies," the lightkeeper's granddaughter remembers. "They never bothered to cut them and in the late afternoon you would see them heading back to the city with huge bundles of the lilies covering their backs. Long before World War I they were becoming scarce, and finally there were only a few here and there. The huge patches of blue were no longer to be seen. In fact, most of the wildflowers were devastated in the same way by hikers. They would gather the flowers as they hiked along and discard them because they wilted." In selected areas on the reservation, native iris and lilies survive to this day, with new-found respect after generations of careless gatherings.

The isolation of Fort Point also produced some imaginative games for the children and their flowers. The massive 7 ft. thick, brick fortress, with its open, interior courtyard three stories high, was, and is, a perfect setting for sailing, as Mrs. Nagel remembers. "We used to pick the flowers from the marguerite bush and sail them down into the court of the fort."

The gun emplacements failed to intimidate the young children; Mrs. Nagel vividly recalls the drifting sand and candytuft, poppies "and other flowers" that shrouded the large firing stations. Fort Point, unlike its architectural relative at Fort Sumter, South Carolina, has never fired a shot, has only a peaceful, playful, plentiful history, not unlike the history of the city in which it rests today. The fortifications by San Francisco Bay wait once again for visitors to see the flowers and the surf, the gun emplacements and the settled sand.

Early Alcatraz Island view of its Army post with tennis court, cannon ball edging, and formal gardens up against Citadel in 1893. Prison cellblock sits on the site of the tennis court and garden today. Cannon balls were later sold for scrap. (Courtesy National Maritime Museum, San Francisco)

Tricyclists and bugler survey the sweep of cannon balls which adorned private and public gardens on the Presidio, and other San Francisco posts, in the 1890s. Note successful tree planting results. (Courtesy National Archives)

Cannon balls surround flower beds on the Presidio in this 1905 photograph. (Courtesy Ft. Point and Army Museum Association)

Officers' gardens spilled down the sheltered hill of Fort Mason (then Point San Jose) in the 1800s, as today. Three of the houses survive. This view looking west shows mounds of sand, near left, near the site of the Maritime Museum and Ghirardelli Square today. (Courtesy National Maritime Museum, San Francisco)

Out where the cliffs take a turn to the south, and the ocean waves break below, a 21-acre estate huddles against the wind, as it did a century ago. Somehow escaping as a military encampment, this stretch of shoreline, Sutro Heights, was once the most elaborate garden in the city. The seals bark as they did a hundred years ago, the wind howls as ever before, but little remains of the Victorian garden created here by San Francisco's premier plantsman, Adolph Sutro.

The cypress, pine and palm trees, planted a hundred years ago to break the wind, are towering and awkward, obliterating the sun from the once-magnificent flower beds below. Today, across the way, hundreds of tourists shop and dine at the Cliff House (which Mr. Sutro once owned), unaware of the fragile, decaying beauty immediately above the shore.

Hundreds of roses bloomed along Palm Avenue where carriages clipped along in the Sutro Heights heyday of the 1880s and 1890s. Exotic flora filled the enormous glass conservatory, and messages carved from mounds of colorful flowers greeted visitors to the promontory. President Harrison came, as did San Franciscans, en masse, to see the elaborate concoction some called "Sutro's Folly."

Created in the early 1880s by the flamboyant and energetic Mr. Sutro—who amassed his fortune tunneling through silver mines in the Sierra Nevadas,—the garden opened to rave press reviews in 1885. While Adolph Sutro was mayor of the city, in the 1890s, the garden was in its prime.

Rather than choose an in-town residential site, as his contemporaries did, Mr. Sutro picked this outlying seaside site for its splendid garden potential—21 acres was a vast city estate even then. The modest 'cottage' on the grounds remained, with few alterations, during Mr. Sutro's lifetime, and until 1939, when the wrecker's ball demolished the memories.

His planned botanical library materialized, but not on Sutro Heights, as he planned—"Too foggy and damp by the sea," his friends advised. Instead, the collection shifted from site to site before finding a permanent home five miles south and a mile inland, above Lake Merced. But half of his rare book collection, temporarily housed in a downtown warehouse, perished in the 1906 earthquake and fire; had the entire collection been stored at Sutro Heights, it, too, would be on view today at the Sutro State Library on Winston Drive.

He traveled extensively in search of plants and botanical manuscripts for his garden and library; his acquisition, at London auction in 1886, of several volumes of British botanist Sir Joseph Banks' papers guaranteed that scholars, too, would travel great distances a century later to study these and other rare documents—65,000 volumes—at the Sutro Library. Correspondence and herbariums accumulated by early British and American plant explorers round out the extensive Sutro collection.

Adolph Sutro, dapper and proud of his "Sutro Heights" floral plaque, 1880s.
(Courtesy Sutro State Library, San Francisco)

The carriage entrance to Sutro Heights, with palms and other exotics lining the roadway into the Heights. This southwest-facing avenue is intact, but overgrown, today. (Courtesy Sutro State Library, San Francisco)

Opposite. Sutro Heights Conservatory, 1900, flanked by statues and other stone adornments scattered everywhere on the lawns. (Courtesy Strybing Arboretum Society)

In the giddy aftermath of gold and silver discoveries, San Franciscans in the late 1800s gouged the city's eastern hills to fill the bayshore, but ignored the sand dunes that smothered the western shoreline six miles away, at the site of Mr. Sutro's garden. Having carved an impossible tunnel through the mountains years earlier, Mr. Sutro summoned his engineering skills to water and house his precious plant collection, and to conquer the shifting sands.

He was persistent—or stubborn, depending on who judged this self-made millionaire—in designing the garden himself. Within four years of purchasing the barren site, thousands of plant specimens were in place, ready for the grand opening. He employed dozens of gardeners to keep the carpets of flowers ship-shape, and to tend the seedlings in his conservatory on the hill.

He succeeded in luring the masses to his ornate garden, to show them the plant introductions that would soon make their mark by the sea. Sutro Heights had all the follies and trappings of the pretentious Victorian era: stone statues, glass enclosures, carpet bedding and vistas at the end of each long view.

The almost circus-like atmosphere cloaked his serious intent, to create the most beautifully landscaped garden in the city. Hoping to surpass the architectural curiosities sprouting on Nob and Rincon Hills, he spared no expense in procuring the best, and the most, plant material and in sharing his seedlings with the city's schoolchildren. His introduced eucalyptus trees stand tall (and continue invading native brush) on the mountain that bears his name in the heart of this city, and on nearby Mt. Davidson. He owned the mountain, as well as vast portions of the westernmost sand dunes, the unwanted land in the great San Francisco outback, four miles west of Nob Hill. At one point, he owned more than one tenth of San Francisco.

Unlike Queen Victoria, however, this Victorian curiosity lasted but a brief moment; Mr. Sutro died within a decade of his garden's grand opening, and the horse and buggy set soon switched allegience to a 1,000 acre marvel springing up in the sand dunes beneath Sutro Heights—the curiosity called Golden Gate Park. The turn of the century ushered in the era of grand municipally-owned parks in San Francisco, so private follies like Sutro Heights, along with Woodward's Gardens and others in the warm Mission District, faded from view, if not from memory.

And today, on a grander scale still, the United States government has recently purchased Sutro Heights from the city with promises of a gradual return to its past glory. If Mayor Sutro was still around, he would certainly insist on telling the President how best to lay out and plant that garden by the sea.

Sutro Heights floral plaque, 1889. (Courtesy Sutro State Library, San Francisco)

Sutro, in top hat, left, with his staff of gardeners, Sutro Heights, 1880s. (Courtesy Sutro State Library, San Francisco)

The parapet and paraphernalia, including statues of children and mushrooms, adorning the top of Sutro Heights. The stone wall is the only remnant of past glory. (Courtesy Sutro State Library, San Francisco)

Pacific Ocean view, from Sutro Heights, looking south. (Courtesy Strybing Arboretum Society)

Sutro Heights today, with Marin hills beyond.

*The Gold Rush
Brings the
Settlers*

Silver and gold, fish and fruits, all in abundance, contributed to the early wealth of San Francisco, in the two decades before the overland railroad linked San Francisco with the rest of the country. While the Spanish viewed foreign traders with suspicion, American settlers, after winning the territory from Mexico in 1846, set about opening up borders and horizons.

The northeast portion of the city, the original village then called Yerba Buena, has handsome squares, set aside early and surviving to this day. **Portsmouth Square,** on the northern edge of the Financial District today, was, in the early years of the village, the center of the city's activity. The shoreline came within inches of "The Plaza" as it was then named. Few Spanish residents live near the square today; Orientals jam the little square, now placed over a parking garage, to play board games and practice graceful t'ai-chi ch'uan here on the edge of crowded Chinatown.

Equidistant north and south of historic Portsmouth Square—a 10 or 15 minute walk in either direction—lie two more squares, both set aside in 1850 by the city's first mayor, John White Geary. Two years after dedicating these squares, and leaving his permanent stamp on this city, Mayor Geary returned to his native Pennsylvania, where he served as governor from 1867 to 1873.

Union Square, the southernmost square, is today lined with regal palms presiding over pigeons and people, in that order. Union sympathizers gathered here for speechmaking in the 1860s, hence, its name. Redesigned by architect Timothy Pflueger (whose streamlined I. Magnin building anchors the southeast corner of the park) in the early 1940s, the park was elevated above an underground parking garage, quite a modern concept at the time. The sophisticated shopping district surrounding the park is as viable today as earlier this century.

Union Square, in the heart of the downtown shopping district, set aside in 1850. This 1941 view, looking north, shows the park before it was torn up for an underground car park. The people and pigeons returned when the construction crew finished, and continue to populate the park today. Cable car, upper left, ready to climb to Nob Hill in the distance. (Photo by Gabriel Moulin Studios, courtesy Pflueger Architects, San Francisco)

At the foot of Telegraph Hill, seven blocks north of the Financial District, is the second park—**Washington Square**—set aside within two years of the gold strike. It soon became a magnet for waves of immigrants who settled in the surrounding neighborhood. In this sunny valley between Russian and Telegraph Hills, warm greetings were exchanged in foreign (until recently, Italian) tongues, giving this North Beach park an international tone. Orientals outnumber Italians in some quarters near the park today.

These three original squares serve their purpose well a century after their set-aside. Intended as refuges in a rapidly-expanding city, the scale remains the same while the style of each square is dissimilar in every way. Two are now built over underground automobile garages, making access to the parks more difficult; the third, Washington Square, is at street level—and always will be, if Telegraph Hill history repeats itself when the idea surfaces again down at City Hall.

South Park was, and is, an oval greensward, and another early example of pioneer vision—this time, by an Englishman, George Gordon. Taking his cue from Berkeley Square in London, this land developer laid out a similar grass oval in 1856, but his ambitious scheme for London-type townhouses fizzled after the decline of the posh neighborhood in the 1870s. Surrounded by industrial development, small-scale South Park today is enjoying a renaissance as the business district (and its office workers seeking sun mid-day) edges toward this isolated oasis.

The city grew so rapidly and haphazardly, however, most early settlers had little time for long-range vision. Finally, the decision-makers, at the urging of businessmen and newspaper editorials, called for outside help in laying out the city and in plotting the parks. They summoned an Easterner, who had recently visited the West, a man whose reputation for integrity of landscape design would shape East Coast cities and, later, the West. Only a decade earlier, he had laid out Central Park, reclaiming a swamp and sewage pit in the process. San Francisco, impressed, sent its official plea to the esteemed firm of Olmsted, Vaux & Company on November 17, 1865.

Washington Square, at the foot of Telegraph Hill, in February bloom. Set aside in 1850 by Mayor John Geary, surrounded by an international mix of residents, the park is well used. Its southwest corner was sliced off for roadmaking in the late 1800s, and reappears across Columbus Avenue as a tiny remnant from the original square.

The letter arrived on February 26, 1866, three months later. Frederick Law Olmsted replied: "It is obvious that San Francisco differs from other towns which have provided themselves with parks, in the incompleteness of its general plan. . . ." The newness, the incomplete plans proved to be San Francisco's greatest assets in forming its permanent character.

By the 1860s, cities in the east, and abroad, had absorbed most of their useable land, Mr. Olmsted reminded the San Francisco policymakers. Only the dregs—or financially worse, the already-developed land—remained for park pickings. "Boston, to extend her public-grounds, is obliged to fill up the back bay, there being no other direction in which such an improvement can be made. . . .Philadelphia is in a similar quandary; and having eight years ago acquired a small, inconveniently situated, and very imcomplete park, is laying over from year to year the question of a more adequate arrangement." Time was money and both were in short supply.

"San Francisco has a future more certain than any of these older towns, and its probable requirements are more easily to be anticipated," Mr. Olmsted enthused. However, San Francisco's past, in the eyes of Frederick Law Olmsted, was as bleak as the future was bright.

The landscape architect disapproved of the San Francisco of the 1860s. "The most popular place of resort for pleasure-seekers . . . is a burial ground on a high elevation, scourged by the wind, laid out only with regard to the convenience of funerals, with no trees or turf. . . . I have, more than once, seen workingmen resort with their families to enjoy a pic-nic in the shelter of the tomb-stones, and hundreds every fine day make it the beginning and end of an effort at healthful recreation."

The people of easy circumstances, and the "spendthrifts" could ride their buggies over the sand dunes to the beach, or visit the racecourse, and the young boys could always take to the streets or wharves, "but the women and girls will, as a rule, neither find their nerves tranquilized, nor their strength invogorated, nor their tastes improved by any recreation that is open to them in the streets or in any of the public places which have been so far established," Mr. Olmsted scolded.

Given the great wealth of this city from its inception, the state of the city in the 1860s was, to him, "not merely disgraceful and shocking to all sense of propriety—barbarous and barbarizing—but it is positively wasteful and destructive of the sources of wealth and prosperity possessed by the city."

One final bit of advice, before he got down to specifics, must have swayed the decision-makers. "It is . . . important to remember that a public pleasure ground, when once formed within a city, possesses a character of permanency beyond any civic building, and usually becomes the most unchangeable feature in its plan."

Four years later, in 1870, Golden Gate Park was carved out of the sand dunes, its permanence implanted on maps and minds. The road builders, the monument and stadium builders have all taken their slice of the park, with automobiles, and accompanying roadway intrusions, the greatest lingering threat to Golden Gate Park.

Elegant, large (four times larger than the combined downtown squares), residential squares were similarly set aside in the city's north quadrant, and today stand as cool hilltop enclaves surrounded by handsome homes and apartments. The squares of Pacific Heights enhance their hilltops and add to the elegance of their neighborhoods, as does Alamo Square to its surrounds, blocks south.

Alamo Square, surrounded by wood-carved Victorian homes, is the picture postcard scene commonly photographed with the downtown skyline on the eastern horizon. When the neighborhood rebounded after years of decline, an address on the square was the first sought. An address *in* the square, however, was the prime objective of one "Dutch Charlie" Duane who claimed the parkland was his own, and until 1877 successfully beat back city efforts to take the park for the public.

The view from Alamo Square to **Alta Plaza** is as clear today as the park-makers intended; the 12-acre open hilltops, with the bay view to the north, opens up unexpected vistas in the center of the city. Most likely, the early settlers, on horseback—making their way from Mission Dolores to the northern ridges of the Presidio—found the high ground and its water first; tradition paved the way for the permanent open land enjoyed today.

But first, the quarrymen had their turn at Alta Plaza, leaving it in ruins. John McLaren worked his magic with this park, as he already had in Golden Gate Park. He filled in the quarry with rubbish, then hauled in topsoil, and planted grass and flowers after laying out paths and tennis courts. The grand stairway on the south side of the park is said to be a copy of a grand staircase outside a Monte Carlo gaming casino.

The design of Alta Plaza is perhaps the most eye-catching of any of the squares; the mansions that line the perimeter add to its beauty of place. The hilltop plaza, however, narrowly escaped real estate development in the 1930s when the city attorney ruled in favor of the preservationists.

On a knoll four blocks east of Alta Plaza, separated by a dip in the landscape, **Lafayette Square** stands as a monument to one man's perseverance, to one man's insistence that observatories and mansions belong on hilltops, rather than uninvited riff-raff. Sam Holladay held out for years, entertaining the city's literary elite in his white mansion on the hill that informally bore his name, Holladay's Hill (or Holladay Heights). The massive hedging on the south, the wonderful view from the height of the hill, the mysterious apartment enclave carved through the eastern end of the park, the disappearing staircases, add to its allure.

32

Alamo Square, looking east over Victorian rooftops toward spectacular skyline view, December. The square is in public ownership over the protests of Dutch Charlie Duane, who claimed the land as his own in the 1800s.

Alta Plaza, between Alamo Square and San Francisco Bay, was set aside early, but used for quarrying before John McLaren filled in the eyesore and created the grand staircases descending the hill. The most eye-catching of the hilltop squares.

On paper, at least, dozens of other parks emerged in the early days of the city—the oval of Holly Park, the craggy expanse of Buena Vista Park, 12-acre Lobos Square, now Moscone, on the sand flats across from Fort Mason, the narrow nameless 'public square' south of Mountain Lake in the Presidio. (Noticably absent from early plans were some of today's most popular magnets—Coit Tower and park on Telegraph Hill and Huntington Park on Nob Hill).

All of these squares were set aside well before the turn of the century, long before city planning became a profession, by a band of civic-minded pioneers, dedicated to a city beautiful. Adolph Sutro kept his eye on the growing western half of the city, buying up land and planting groves of trees that survive to this day. His successor in office, Mayor (later, Senator) James Duvall Phelan dedicated his life to the city beautiful movement, convincing his contemporaries to part with their money for parks, boulevards and grand designs in the eastern, crowded quadrant, five miles east of Sutro Heights.

At the turn of the century, businessmen formed the Association for the Improvement and Adornment of San Francisco to put finishing touches on a final city design. With Golden Gate Park in place, the businessmen turned to Chicago architect Daniel Hudson Burnham to draw a grand plan for San Francisco.

While the land was undulating and unpopulated, the vision was easier to carry out; and because it was carried out at a time when the city was young and forward-looking, San Francisco, to this day, is as civilized and open to the sky as any city could want, a century after incorporation.

Lafayette Square, the third 'Western Addition' hilltop set aside in the 1800s, is a short walk from Alta Plaza. The park commands a fine view of San Francisco Bay to the north, and the city's central hills to the southwest, pictured here.

At dawn on April 18, 1906, San Francisco and its design were radically and permanently altered. Only months before, the great Chicago architect, Daniel Burnham, at the invitation of former Mayor James Duvall Phelan, and others, had submitted his elaborate plan for the adornment of San Francisco.

From his elevated vantage point, in a make-shift office on Twin Peaks, Mr. Burnham surveyed the young city and laid out long boulevards radiating from central circular drives and fanning out over hills and through valleys. He and his able assistant Edward H. Bennett drew dramatic parallels between San Francisco and ancient cities well designed. The scale was grand. The Burnham Plan was buried in the rubble of City Hall on that beautiful spring morning in 1906 and post-earthquake efforts, particularly those of architect Willis Polk, to revive portions of the plan, failed.

In later years, some of the 4,000 acres of parks recommended by Burnham for public ownership materialized, but a great deal was lost to development. He suggested two hilltop greenbelts radiating from the central hills south west and east. "In case of a great conflagration, this system of parks and connecting parkways would form an effective barrier to its spread . . ." he prophecized, all too accurately, a year before the great fire.

With John McLaren nudging the city architect, most of the hilltops and creek beds were included for future park purchase. The park Panhandle stretched the distance between City Hall and Golden Gate Park; one of the great losses in the buried plan. The entire top of Potrero Hill—the size of the whole of Buena Vista Park—was recommended for inclusion in the city park system, and a magnificent meandering Islais Creek Park came off the drawing board, with elaborate stone adornments, where today the Southern Freeway cuts across the city. Neither suggestion survived.

The parks, those that existed in 1906, played a major role in rejuvenating the city in despair. In some areas, the only patch of land free from fallen rubble, the greenswards became home to thousands of San Franciscans in the aftermath of the earthquake and fire that followed.

The two major open areas, the Presidio and Golden Gate Park, and dozens of small neighborhood squares, served as temporary living quarters for displaced San Franciscans who would otherwise have fled the city. The children continued their schooling, uninterrupted in outdoor classrooms while parents

Daniel Burnham's suggested design treatment for Telegraph Hill. Mr. Burnham's fanciful 1905 sketches intimidated some San Franciscans at the time. The 1906 earthquake, however, effectively ended dialogue on the Burnham Plan, despite revival efforts. (Courtesy College of Environmental Design, University of California, Berkeley)

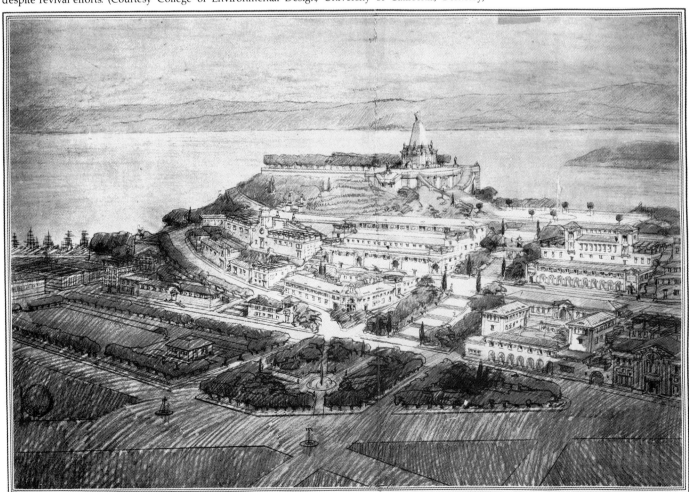

While the hills were still bare, and the vistas unimpeded, Daniel Burnham envisioned everything but chariot races in this Atheneum, snug in its Twin Peaks setting overlooking the Pacific. The arena never materialized on the hill although more humble sporting enclosures are scattered in the valleys of San Francisco today.
(Courtesy College of Environmental Design, University of California, Berkeley)

tended to the more immediate task of rebuilding their homes and the city. The bond, for many, was unbroken, in large measure thanks in part to well-placed squares and parks, in part to efficient military participation from a home base within the city, and in part to the close-knit social fabric.

Former Mayor (and later State Senator) James Duvall Phelan, the champion of the City Beautiful Movement, watched helplessly as his mansion and beautiful garden near Mission Dolores went up in flames after the earthquake. A spark from his singed cypress hedge leapfrogged across his estate and within hours, his possessions and lovely orchard and garden lay in ruins. In his memoirs, he recounts—with much pride—how he found a fine camping spot in Golden Gate Park between the Japanese Tea Garden and de Young Museum, where trees and water protected and nourished his temporarily wounded spirit.

Across town, near the crest of Nob Hill, Alice Eastwood awoke in her two-room rented flat and thought nothing of the early morning shake; Nob Hill foundations are embedded in solid rock. But on the mud flats of Market Street below Nob Hill, where the Academy of Sciences housed Alice Eastwood's botanical collection, and others, the buildings crumbled to the ground or precariously leaned against one another in the hours after the earthquake.

The story of Alice Eastwood's perserverance in the next few hours, of her determination to save the Academy specimens while her personal possessions sat vulnerable to fire in her Nob Hill apartment, is an extraordinary example of San Francisco pluck. She commandeered a cart and a young lawyer to help her lower specimens from the sixth floor offices (the marble stairs leading to the upper floors had caved in, but the bannister, alongside, provided footing for passage), then hauled the wrapped collection to a house of a friend, Reverand Joseph Worcester, on Russian Hill. As flames approached that hill, the Academy collection was hand carted down the Russian Hill goat path to a safer sanctuary of another friend, Captain Hahn, at Fort Mason.

Her single-minded devotion to the Academy herbarium stands out today as exemplory, but at the time, Alice Eastwood's fame was for her botanical prowess, in an era when young women were not yet accepted in all professions. Her early (until 1892) Denver botanizing provided the nucleus of the herbarium at the University of Colorado, and her 1893 *Popular Flora of Denver* is a slim but invaluable reference to the early Denver landscape.

South Park stood alone in the rubble south of Market after the earthquake. The army kept order from quarters here and elsewhere in the stricken city. Note singed but surviving trees standing in the park. (Courtesy San Francisco Public Utilities Commission, photo archives)

Refugees camped in Lobos (now Moscone) Square, with Fort Mason encampment to the northeast. (Courtesy National Maritime Museum, San Francisco)

Looking Toward Alcatraz Island from Nob Hill, San Francisco,
Russian Hill at Right, April, 1906
Greatest Fire on Record. $400,000,000 Damage Done—$395,000,000 by
Fire.   Damage by Earthquake Nominal.

I lived on the street to the right of the one shown in the picture.
Alice.

613   'WOOD'S'', PUBLISHERS, LOS ANGELES

Alice Eastwood, pictured in 1912. While lecturing abroad, audiences,
Miss Eastwood noted, were eager to learn about California plants—
and all about the San Francisco earthquake of 1906. Her expertise in
both matters made her a popular guest during her post-earthquake
travels.
(Courtesy California Academy of Sciences, San Francisco)

Alice Eastwood's poignant postcard to relatives in Denver tells the
story of destruction of 1906. The Academy of Sciences botany
specimens, saved by Miss Eastwood, were rushed to the Russian Hill
enclave, pictured here, while fire engulfed other Academy collections downtown.
(Courtesy California Academy of Sciences, San Francisco)

Immediately after the earthquake, Miss Eastwood studied and traveled in the East and abroad
before coming home to San Francisco. Her diaries of those years, 1907–1911, modestly reveal her worldwide acclaim: dinner at the White House in Washington with the Merriams and President Roosevelt,
study at the National Herbarium, reception at the home of Alexander Graham Bell. Her Cambridge,
Massachusetts, stay included study at the Gray Herbarium "looking up plants that for years I had longed
to see." She published—in Latin, as was necessary then—and named new plants, then set out for
Thoreau's Walden Pond, but came away "terribly disappointed." Cranberry bogs and "original Concord
grapes" added to the Massachusetts allure for this botanist.

In England, Kew Gardens, and its scientific studies, became the focus for her stay, but one engage-
ment stood out above all others—an invitation to luncheon at the home of then 94-year-old Sir Joseph
Hooker in Surrey. He proudly showed Miss Eastwood his garden, pointing out "a very good specimen of
California chinquapin which he himself had planted when he retired [from Kew] about 30 years
before."

California, at that time, was utopia to a keen plantsman, California was the new plant fronier just
beginning to be tapped. Miss Eastwood was the cultivated connection, and the British treated her like
royalty. The gardeners on the estates she visited in Britain, however, were hardly aware of her royal
status. When she commented on a "magnificent sequoia" growing at Warwick Castle, the castle gardener
"corrected me, saying, no, that is a wellingtonia."

38

Alice Eastwood's later garden, on Russian Hill, was filled with fuchsias and clematis, although she was more enthusiastic about other people's plants and gardens.
(Photo Imogen Cunningham, courtesy California Academy of Sciences, San Francisco)

Back in San Francisco, she became Curator of Botany at the California Academy of Sciences, and held the post for 57 years, advising John McLaren, his Golden Gate Park gardeners and anyone else whose curiousity was aroused by a beautiful plant in or near San Francisco. She was the founding member and spark behind creation of the beguiling Shakespeare Garden, then known as the Garden of Shakespeare's Flowers. Her inspiration had come from her trip abroad, and her Academy office over-looked the shaded glade which now holds a bust of the bard, inscriptions from his works, and flowers to illustrate his words.

Alice Eastwood and James Duvall Phelan together with other pioneering San Franciscans con-tributed to this city's rich horticultural archives and immense pride of place. Later, when individual undertaking gave way to the more extensive designs of real estate developers and engineers, the city took on a more massive scale, more complicated pace; but the pioneering promise continues, ever so quietly and deeply, in the souls of San Franciscans today.

Out of the ashes came the rebuilding, and in some cases, the deeding of forlorn property to the city. **Huntington Park,** on the crest of Nob Hill, is one such example of family generosity in the aftermath of disaster. Arabella Huntington gave the hilltop site, a full half block, to the city, with the proviso that the park be reserved for children and their attendants.

Whether Mrs. Huntington's lawyers, or the city's, wisely withdrew that condition, is uncertain, but today, this handsome, urbane square sits serenely in the shadow of a cathedral and posh hotels and men's club. The brownstone mansion which houses the men's Pacific Union Club and shares the crest of Nob Hill with Huntington Park, has a flowering year-round garden on the California Street side, next door to, and plainly seen from, the park. The salvia seems never to quit, as it proudly stands above the bronze fence, and the trees against the pink-hued stone are spectacular in bloom. Even the fall color of the vines lingers against the western boundary line and gives a hint of the changing seasons, and the rains yet to come.

In the years that followed the earthquake, planning the city became a bits-and-pieces process, and the city relied on citizen generosity more than ever before. Mrs. Sigmund Stern, Carl E. Larsen, Walter S. Johnson and others donated land and contributed as much to the city shape as did all the paper plans. But the 1915 Panama-Pacific Exposition—The Fair—captured the city at a vulnerable moment and picked up spirits as much as anything else after the earthquake.

Acre upon acre (635) of enormous buildings, surrounded by dazzling gardens, stretching along the northern waterfront—filled for the occasion—and gave San Franciscans pause to cheer the Panama Canal and the rebuilding of the city. The fair was a new beginning, a toast to the days ahead, rather than the days gone by. The Palace of Fine Arts is a regal reminder of the 1915 Fair, and the Marina Green is a waterside remnant, one of the most heavily-used parks in the city today. Neither were handed down without controversy, however, as preservationists battled the land grabbers for the prizes. The whole of the **Marina** District, with its bright stucco houses and apartments facing the shore, and its neatly clipped Italian gardens, sits today on the site of the 1915 Fair.

On the other end of town, in 1915, a Scotsman named Duncan McDuffie was struggling, financially, with a visionary residential development named **St. Francis Wood.** The planted boulevards leading

Huntington Park in autumn, with highrise hotels and Pacific Union Club beyond.

to and around water fountains in line with the sea, the private parks hidden mid-block, the bold architectural entry gates, all were placed according to plan. McDuffie, a dedicated conservationist who would later become president of the Sierra Club and have a redwood grove named in his honor, hired the best talent of the day to design his in-town residential park.

Olmsted Brothers, landscape architects of Massachusetts, laid out the St. Francis Wood street pattern and plantings (and at least one garden, see The Early Days, private gardens) and even recommended beginning anew when the main boulevard proved too narrow in size. Architects John Galen Howard and Henry H. Gutterson designed the imposing entry gates and fountains which today set this enclave apart from the high-speed thoroughfares surrounding it.

One of the first improvements completed to lure prospective buyers was the quaint little diamond-shaped park, with trelliswork protecting newly-planted bulbs. The eucalyptus had hardly been cut down, the gophers had hardly been chased out, before the garden went in.

Reminiscing in a speech to his homeowner's group years after the War (which effectively shut down development sales), Duncan McDuffie thanked those who made St. Francis Wood possible: ". . . the nursery and planting staff, not forgetting the official lamp-lighter, gopher catcher and gardener extraordinary to many of the residents of St. Francis Wood, the irrepressible, delightful and loyal Angelo Celestre."

In the Angelo Celestre tradition, the gardening staff of St. Francis Wood today maintains the pretty parks and gardens, although lamp lighting is no longer necessary.

In nearby **Forest Hill,** developed at about the same time, gardener Tom Sershen carries on the tradition of gardening in that part of the city. As designed by Mark Daniels, the curving streets are lined with trees and shrubs, and maintained at quality standard today, in part because the homeowners keep the gardening tradition alive through special assessment, although, at one time, five gardeners kept Forest Hill in flower. The acre garden surrounding the Forest Hill Clubhouse is particularly lovely in spring, when the rhododendrons are in bloom.

Sea Cliff, also designed by Mark Daniels, is less wooded, in part because this area escaped Adolph Sutro's ambitious tree-planting in the 1880s, in part because the palms planted cast less shade, when young, than eucalyptus and pines. Sited on a bluff immediately above the sea, the homes are in direct path of winds and fog from the water, but have some of the best views in the city. The gardens are walled off by glass enclosures and are full of vibrant geraniums and roses.

A proposed development plan for the outer Richmond, presented to the Sutro heirs, but never realized in its entirety. The bluffs are preserved in public ownership, and Sutro Heights park, left, also survives. (Sketch by W. H. Bull, courtesy Sutro State Library, San Francisco)

Sea Cliff shelters one of the two best beaches on the San Francisco shore; understandably, the neighborhood was reluctant to give it up for public use, but, in 1933, the city won its battle to claim China Beach. The city failed, however, to convince the public that this beach be named for the generous citizen who donated $50,000 (a great sum at the time) toward its purchase. The James D. Phelan Memorial Beach just didn't roll off the tongue as easily as China Beach, which is remembered as the cove where Chinese sailors found refuge. The sea fig and tamarisk and wild roses that have managed to take hold on the sandy hillside mark an efficient and elegant path to the water.

Sally Woodbridge eloquently captures the architecture of each emerging San Francisco neighborhood in her book, *Architecture, San Francisco*. Underlying the city's growth, however, was a taste and style which sometimes slipped from grace but usually managed to redeem itself in the end. The scarring of Mt. Davidson, but the wildflower preserve on top; the uninterrupted Sunset grid, yet the cool Stern Grove and Sunset Heights Park bring class to the perimeter; the high-speed roadway within inches of Lake Merced, yet the stunning golf courses adding beauty beyond.

Not until the 1970s were the remaining hilltops and irretrievable lands permanently set aside. As time passed, hilltops had become harder to acquire and nail down—Telegraph Hill was an early struggle against the quarrymen, making the remaining hills vulnerable as never before. Help come from unexpected quarters: the city's planning director, Allan Jacobs, led the way after writing an open space plan, then insisting it be implemented. His vision and perserverance are most recent gifts to the city.

The future is in the hands of the taste-makers and decision makers; perhaps, if history repeats itself, the two will join forces for the continued beauty of the city.

Adolph Sutro's planted trees, here at Anza and 47th Avenue, stand in contrast to the early Richmond District landscape of sand dunes and spring wildflowers. The Pacific Ocean pounds the shore, below this hill. (Courtesy Sutro State Library, San Francisco)

The Marina Green, on the city's northern shoreline, is on land filled in for the 1915 Panama-Pacific Exposition. Mansions line the green, facing the Bay, and at Christmas create quite a show of greens and lights in clipped front gardens. The Marina Green has few trees, allowing sun into this popular park. (Courtesy Barbara Stauffacher-Solomon)

The Palace of Fine Arts, and duck pond, also survive from the 1915 Exposition. Efforts to move the relic and tear it down failed.

The original garden at St. Francis Wood, a neighborhood laid out by the Olmsted Brothers of Brookline, Massachusetts in the early 1900s. The first St. Francis Wood gardener, Angelo Celestre, listed lamplighting and gopher-chasing among his many outdoor chores. The neighborhood still maintains a gardening staff to keep the public gardens pretty. (Courtesy College of Environmental Design, documents collection, University of California, Berkeley)

FROM AN ARTICLE IN HARPER'S MONTHLY
FOR JULY, 1924, ENTITLED

"*San Francisco Revisited*"

By KATHERINE FULLERTON GEROULD

"An unobstructible view is a marvelous thing and when, as at Sea Cliff, you are set down on the very edge of the ocean, and own the whole tumble of rock and earth down to the very waves of the Pacific—so that none can ever take from you the vision of the Golden Gate, the open ocean and the rose-pink mountains of Contra Costa opposite—you are willing to pay a great deal of money for your lot, if the money is to be had."

"At Sea Cliff you wall off your little garden with glass, to fend off the sea winds, and sit in a hooded bath-chair among the giant pansies. The fact of the automobile can work both ways—making it easy for you to dwell within the city limits, as well as bringing the country nearer."

This brochure, and the sea, lured prospective homebuyers to Sea Cliff in the 1920s. Today, many Sea Cliff gardens are enclosed in glass, as the promoters intended. (Courtesy David and Howard Allen, Belvedere Land Company)

45

Popular hiking trails around Lake Merced in the 1920s. Condominiums, golf courses and high speed roads take their place today.
(Photo courtesy San Francisco Public Utilities Commission, photo archives)

The sand dunes, near Lake Merced, 1924. (Courtesy San Francisco Public Utilities Commission, photo archives)

An overview of Lake Merced in 1925. A public golf course now crosses the center of the natural lake. (Courtesy San Francisco Public Utilities Commission, photo archives)

Below. The southwestern city landscape in 1925, before the Olympic Golf Club turned the sand dunes into fairways. (Courtesy San Francisco Public Utilities Commission, photo archives)

Adolph Spreckels built these flower beds in the middle of this Pacific Heights street, to slow and silence automobile traffic on the hillside beside his mansion. The less wealthy just put up with the sputtering machines making their mark in the city during the 1920s.

Carl Henry lavished attention and money on his Russian Hill garden at Hyde and Lombard in the early 1900s. Seen from the Chestnut Street side, looking south, this 1919 view shows terraces and tulips sweeping down the Hyde Street hill. His dream of donating this garden to the city faded when his (Owl Drug) fortune dwindled; the property sold in 1937. Cable car line runs alongside the property, right, and "crooked" Lombard Street, which was then steep and straight, bordered the south garden.

48

The
Private Gardens
Flourish

Gardening has always been, for San Franciscans, a remarkably simple endeavor at least when compared to coastal gardening elsewhere. Hardy plants from former homelands flourished for early American settlers in San Francisco alongside exciting new, tender, plants, brought in on ships from Australia, New Zealand and the Pacific coast of South America. Enthusiastic importers—like Charles Abraham of the Western Nursery in Cow Hollow—contributed substantially to the early high standards set for gardens before the turn of the century.

When the West Coast landscape was fresh and unplanted, Ernest H. "Chinese" Wilson of the Arnold Arboretum noted the splendid gardening opportunities awaiting gardeners: "California, of all states in the Union is most favored as a garden region; indeed, I know of no land where the potential possibilities of garden-making are so great," he stated in his book, *If I Were To Make A Garden.* He tracked down, in the Orient, dozens of tender plants that today are seen in many San Francisco gardens, but when he wrote those words, earlier in this century, few of his introductions had established roots on the West Coast.

San Franciscans didn't need convincing, however; gardening as a pursuit and pastime caught on early in the city's history. The year-round mild weather was only one factor contributing to initial successes. The early immigrants—Italians, Scots and Germans particularly—brought their native horticultural skills, but more importantly, continued to practice their craft not only in the city but in the surrounding countryside, which supported farms, orchards and wineries then, as now.

The fashionable early neighborhoods—South Park and Rincon Hill in the 1850s and '60s—had their share of remembered showplaces. Children, those who liked to climb trees, recalled the huge pepper tree overhanging Mr. Sidney Smith's high brick wall on the slope of Rincon Hill, while, near the crest, on Harrison Street, stood the Jerome Lincoln home, with its wide lawns, marble sidewalk and iron hitching post. Ships came to call just below the hill, and often, fresh oranges arrived providing a delicious cargo "full of juice, seeds and sweetness," recalled Alice Hooper McKee, in a report to the San Francisco Garden Club back in 1935. Adventure was right around the corner, and down the hill, then.

Conservatories enjoyed the same status here as elsewhere in the States during the latter half of the last century. Mostly attached to houses, rather than separated from them, the glasshouses served as extensions of the home, as rooms where families gathered after dinner. The men smoked, the children played, and the potted indoor plants—cinerarias, cyclamen, cowslips, and fuchsias—somehow survived the cigars and games.

Climbing plants grew to great heights inside the conservatory, climbers that San Franciscans today plant out-of-doors. "A large heliotrope vine covered one side... intermingled with the delicate star jasmine, then quite common," Anna Beaver told the Garden Club a half century ago. Her family home

Many San Francisco gardens had humble beginnings, on foundations of pure sand, as this Richmond District scene, near 32nd Avenue, shows. (Courtesy Sutro State Library, San Francisco)

and conservatory, at Market and Fifth, long ago disappeared, replaced by office and merchant buildings. Outside the family conservatory, a grass plot ("never called lawn then", according to Miss Beaver) supported the croquet set, the first in the city, perhaps.

Not all glass buildings held potted plants. The huge steam-heated conservatory at Woodward's Gardens—in the sunny, sheltered Mission District—held artifacts and grape vines in addition to new-found exotics. San Franciscans flocked to Woodward's Gardens during its 25-year heydey, between 1868 and 1893.

"Pitcher plants and orchids and tree ferns! It was here that I first saw a Philodendron or Pound Plant, whose rare blossom is said to weigh a pound,"Mr. Woodward's granddaughter, Ethel Malone Brown, remembers. Another pavillion, dramatically sited on the crest of a hill, sheltered a roller skating rink, stage and restaurant, while across the street (near 14th and Mission today), a tunnel led to a zoo and other thrilling attractions. These "gardens", much more than gardens, really, were all the rage elsewhere, but a novelty for this western outpost in the late 1800s.

Each neighborhood had its stamp, its signature. The warm Mission District gardens were full of fruit trees and flowers in the 1870s and '80s. In the gracious James Phelan garden at 17th and Valencia, two blocks east of the original mission settlement, an orchard of cherry trees bore an abundance of fruit, but the figs were the particular favorite of the owner, and proof, to him, of the Mission warmth. A high cypress hedge—"characteristic of such mansions at that time," according to Veronica Kinzie of the Garden Club—enclosed the lawns and rose beds, the heliotrope and lilac bushes.

Nob Hill mansions, in contrast, had few tall hedges enclosing their gardens in the late 1800s. Instead, small patches of lawn, rarely surrounded by massed flowers, led from the ornate doorways to the street just beyond Nob Hill ("Snob Hill" to some) homes, somewhat grander than those in other districts, were nonetheless closer together than Mission estates and Cow Hollow farms. Street trees on Nob Hill were nonexistent, but an occasional palm or evergreen surfaced in the lawn area. Clipped greenery stood against the large homes, as if to protect the walls from the afternoon winds.

The earthquake of 1906 affected private gardens as well as public parks. The refugees, after taking shelter in the city's squares and parks, settled into remote districts between the Presidio and the sea, between the Mission and Lake Merced, so the homeless needed to learn, all over again, which plants might grow in their new microclimates. Once learned, however, gardening in this city entered a fine era, at a time when space and help were abundant, when immigrants eagerly shared their crafts, when new plants poured in, when Golden Gate Park was established in part to educate the masses.

It was a time, in the '20s and '30s, when landscape architecture was coming into its own, yet architects still left their signatures on garden design. A young man named Thomas Church opened his landscape architecture practice in San Francisco, and a Scotsman, John McLaren, just completed a book (at last, a gardening book for San Francisco) called *Gardening in California, Landscape and Flower*.

The 1915 Panama Pacific Exposition was a huge success, and the big trees transplanted there by Mr. McLaren found their way, after the Fair, into private gardens in the city. A magnolia from the Fair went into an enclosed courtyard at the foot of the "Crooked" street on Russian Hill, and dozens of mature trees found a new home along the curved streets of Forest Hill, a new neighborhood at the time. Many trees went back into the parks.

As the city's park superintendant at the time, Mr. McLaren could uproot his own park trees from Golden Gate Park and the Presidio, then park them at the Fair site temporarily. He even transplanted giant yews from nearby cemeteries for the occasion, knowing how easily the tall, somber trees travel from one site to the next.

In the process of laying out the park and the Fair site, Mr. McLaren showed the city how to garden with style, ease and imagination. He also impressed out-of-towners: "What the grand old Nestor of California horticulture, Mr. John McLaren, has accomplished at Golden Gate Park and elsewhere in the vicinity of San Francisco is an indication of the enormous possibilities California possesses. Visitors to the Pan-Pacific Exposition . . . will remember the splendid use . . . of . . . mesembryanthemums . . . created by Mr. John McLaren. . . ." Dr. Wilson boasted in his book.

The freeze of '32 brought out the city's best gardeners for a post-mortem and renewal. The California Horticultural Society emerged from the ruin and has been furthering horticultural pursuits ever since. Years later, the mysterious Helene Strybing gave the city enough money to move an arboretum from the drawing board to reality; today, the popular gardening lectures and demonstrations carry out Mrs. Strybing's wish to educate people about plants and gardening.

Gardens with a Tommy Church stamp, or the stamp of a leading architect, were numerous in the 1930s, '40s and '50s in San Francisco. The prolific Mr. Church, who did more than any other San Franciscan to elevate the status of the new landscape architecture profession, delved into the times and his clients' minds, freely producing streamlined, low maintenance gardens at a time when this view was popular (see March, Tova Wiley garden).

Thomas Church "wanted to bring the outdoors in and the indoors out," gardening teacher Jean Wolff remembers. She also remembers ignoring her own garden—down a steep staircase from the back door—when she was growing up and credits Mr. Church with reawakening an interest in city gardens. His city gardens in San Francisco were, of necessity, a world apart from those he designed immediately to

Trellis mirrored in lily pond sets the 1930s mood in this city garden on Arguello. (Courtesy San Francisco Garden Club)

The Russian Hill garden of Mrs. Horatio P. Livermore, distinguished by its pear orchard and meadow, where tea was often served, on the hard clay soil of this residential hill so near downtown. (Courtesy San Francisco Garden Club)

A sloping Pacific Heights garden, with a 50% grade, on Vallejo Street, smothered in pretty flowers in the 1930s. Pathways, of necessity, cut across, rather than down, the rocky, steep garden. Almost half the gardens in San Francisco slope, to some degree; this example is extreme, and splendid in its execution. (Courtesy San Francisco Garden Club)

A 1930s Thomas Church design in San Francisco garden of Henrietta Moffitt. Clean, clear lines were trademarks of this renowned landscape architect. (Courtesy San Francisco Garden Club)

An early Fort Mason garden, near the site of community garden today. The scale was smaller still, but the gardening challenge just as great, in the windy, treeless city. (Courtesy National Maritime Museum, San Francisco)

the south of the city. The fog and cooler weather meant design changes for San Franciscans—for example, sliding glass doors leading into the garden, a California signature, were not, in Mr. Church's opinion, appropriate for San Francisco gardens, if only because the blast of cold air was so unwelcome.

Jean Wolff's own garden on Telegraph Hill, designed by Mr. Church, remained intact as he envisioned it and stood as a reminder of his design "genius" as Mrs. Wolff recalled. He cared less for plants than design, she remembered, and had his signature plants—mayten tree and agapanthus, among others—to recommend for those gardeners who needed plant advice too.

Mrs. Wolff, however, gave plant advice—and favorite plants—freely to those who would listen and take note. For San Franciscans, she made this timeless statement: "Our summer is usually so windy and cold and nothing does well—I think it's better for people to do easy things very well, like growing geraniums well. You can make a pelargonium look like an azalea actually!" The most essential ingredient for successful city gardening, in the view of Mrs. Wolff, is a carefree and relaxed approach, two characteristics San Franciscans possess in abundance. And once the city gardener relaxes in his garden, Mrs. Wolff knew, the true creativity begins.

While San Franciscans are particularly fortunate in having, preserved, handsome private gardens so near the downtown city core, the public, or street, gardens delight, too, at every turn. Leftover spaces which might be ignored in other cities are adopted, manicured and fussed over by eager San Francisco gardeners. Often, the property is owned by the city or an absentee landlord; ownership and stewardship become blurred when California poppies are at stake.

Fort Mason officers' quarters faced the Bay, sheltered from west winds. General Woodruff and his wife tended this charming garden just before outbreak of the Second World War. Wonderful old plantings, remnants from early gardens, are still evident in the eastern half of the post. (Courtesy San Francisco Garden Club)

A Sea Cliff garden, designed by Gardner Dailey, in the 1930s. (Courtesy San Francisco Garden Club)

Architect Willis Polk, who headed Daniel Burnham's San Francisco office before opening his own practice, designed this Broadway mansion with terrace to match, at a time when architecture and gardens routinely emerged together off the drawing board. (Courtesy San Francisco Garden Club)

Another Willis Polk house and garden, designed together for Mrs. Andrew Welch in 1918. Isabella Worn, who supervised the Filoli plantings, planned the succession of bloom in this town garden. (Courtesy San Francisco Garden Club)

Two ready examples are the dazzling street gardens of Filbert Street on Telegraph Hill, and Lombard Street on Russian Hill, both initiated by single devoted gardeners Grace Marchant and Peter Bercut, respectively. Less well known, but equally impressive, are the Liberty Street gardens above Mission Dolores, cared for by adjacent property owners, and the charming country lanes clinging to hillsides on Bernal Heights. Near the ocean, far from the tourist's eye, are the beautifully manicured steps and fountains of Forest Hill and St. Francis Wood, each maintained by private gardeners, through property owners' special assessment.

San Franciscans excel at street-side gardening, whether on public or private property. But, as any city gardener knows, pretty flowers often disappear in close quarters with passing admirers, so San Franciscans have adapted to this reality with aplomb.

One well-known Marina District garden, for example, which stretches along high-speed Cervantes Boulevard, is a riot of color twice a year and a visual delight for passing motorists on their way to the Golden Gate Bridge, yet the flowers were snatched the moment the spires of snapdragons unfolded. Undaunted, the owner here just left the beds fallow one year, but the neighbors complained bitterly at the absence of the flower show. The following year, in went *short*-stemmed flowers—petunias and the like—which are less enticing for passing pruners, but equally dazzling from afar.

In the warmth of Noe Valley, just west of palm-lined Dolores Street, lies the flower-filled front garden of Rosemary Stewart, a transplanted New Zealander. The ease with which she mixes vines, shrubs and perennials for year-round color on 25th Street hints at the rich gardening heritage New Zealanders bring to San Francisco, in the form of native New Zealand plants and seasoned gardeners.

As a street specimen, the New Zealand Christmas Tree (*Metrosideros*), thrives in the windy Sunset District, while other New Zealand plants take hold in warm seaside areas elsewhere. San Franciscans were slow to plant or accept street trees, for two reasons: the early city landscape held few tall trees, and shade is simply not needed for the heat that rarely comes. While other cities distinguish themselves with their broad tree-lined boulevards and streets, San Francisco instead prides itself on its bright and blue sky, on its long vistas toward the ocean and bay.

The Liberty Street Gardens, above Mission Dolores, are tended by a group of neighbors. Many homeowners plant a small stretch of sunlit garden on the street divider opposite their homes.

The haphazard Bernal Heights street pattern produces wonderful left-overs, handsomely cared for by nearby neighbors. At Powhattan and Wool, this view is to the southwest toward Holly Park, which was one of the first donated parks to the city.

Only recently, Friends of the Urban Forest—a citizen group organized to fill the gap left when tree advocate Brian Fewer left public employ—have convinced a skeptical citizenry that certain trees add to dramatic views, and cast light shade while breaking the wind. Thousands of trees have been planted under the direction of the Friends, who hold street planting parties three weekends out of every four. The Friends cover half the expense of each tree planting, and advise prospective owners on San Francisco's peculiar tree needs.

Public or private, San Francisco gardens are among the best a city might expect. Fortunately for this city, its natural air-conditioning, the fog, chases away heat and pollution, which are two roadblocks to successful city gardening elsewhere. Fortunately, too, settlers come from garden-rich traditions and willingly transplant their acumen to their new soil. San Francisco's deserved reputation as a relaxed and refined city shows in its gardens, just as Charleston's graciousness, New York's sophistication and Boston's traditionalism shows in their town gardens.

Olmsted Brothers designed this St. Francis Wood garden on San Buenaventura. The Olmsted firm also laid out the streets and parkways of the Wood. (Courtesy San Francisco Garden Club)

The Marina District street-side display that dazzles commuters on their way to the Golden Gate Bridge. Neighbors are as attached to this seasonal display as passers-by; flowers mysteriously disappeared until the owner planted only short-stemmed, less pickable, varieties of flowers.

The Noe Valley garden of New Zealander Rosemary Stewart delights passers-by with its year-round flowers. Here, September bloom in the 25th Street garden just west of Dolores.

John McLaren, the Scotsman who planted the park and continued to tame the sand dunes until his death in 1943. (Courtesy Strybing Arboretum Society)

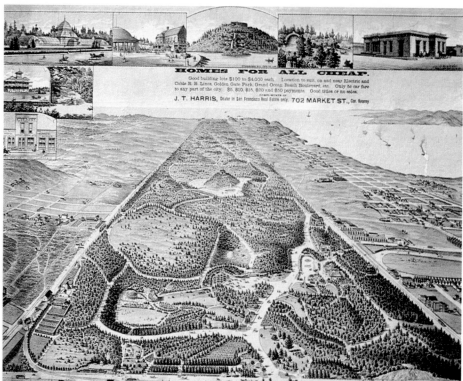

A birds-eye view of the new park, 1892. (Courtesy Strybing Arboretum Society)

III. THE PUBLIC PARKS AND STAIRWAYS

Asking for 100,000 pounds of manure as a birthday present, feisty John McLaren—early, extraordinary superintendant of Golden Gate Park—gave away his secret. He was, to San Franciscans, the man with the golden touch, the man who turned the shifting, lifeless sand dunes into lush meadows and dreamy dells. From 1890 to 1943, he ruled the park, its gardeners and police force with a firm but gentle hand, shaping more than 1,000 city acres for generations to come.

"Uncle John," as he was and is affectionately called, worked wonders with plants and people, at once taming the dunes while extracting promises from politicians and people to support him financially and morally. The park idea got off to a slow start in the 1870s before McLaren showed the town the beauty in their midst.

His longevity contributed to his stature; his longevity also guaranteed an endless supply of Uncle John stories—mostly true though embellished with age. An example: working in the dead of night, just before a damaging roadway was scheduled to slice through his park, he and his crew blocked off access with huge plants placed directly across the proposed right-of-way. He won that one, but lost others, including Kezar Stadium in the 1920s, all concrete occupying a corner of the park once filled with magnificent old rhododendrons.

Rhododendrons and heathers were his favorite plants—fresh bouquets filled his McLaren Lodge office in spring—reminding him of his Scottish heritage and apprentice days at Edinburgh Botanic Gardens. Today, the Rhododendron Dell, so near the great stone lodge he lived (and worked) in more than 40 years, is a memorial, complete with a bronze statue. He reportedly disliked statues, and made every effort to camouflage donated monuments with fast-growing evergreens; the McLaren statue, by sculptor M. Earl Cummings, is, by an odd twist of fate, perhaps the most viewed and photographed piece in the park.

The Scotsman would not likely take the superintendant's job today, old friends note. Faced with a mounting City Hall bureaucracy and paper chase, he would long for the good old days—the days during his long tenure when he ran the park out of a little notebook in his pocket as he made his outdoor rounds, four or five hours *each* day. He knew most every gardener and plant, and spent hardly any time at his desk. His keen sense of apprentice gardeners led to instant promotions for talented newcomers; his on-the-job observations replaced today by point systems and exams.

In winter, in those days, people stayed away in numbers, in part because of the tedious journey to the park. Mr. McLaren and his gardeners used that time to catch up on planting and planning. Today, the park is crowded winter and summer, rain or shine, the year-round gardeners are unionized so midnight forays to block encroaching roadways are out of the question. The park gardeners today enthusiastically carry on Uncle John's work, while park officials tend to the paperwork and politics.

How much did this legendary figure influence the design and planting of the park? A great deal of one, but not the other. The design was pretty much in place before his arrival—his predecessor, William Hammond Hall, is credited with the winding roads that break up the wind and monotony of the 3-mile-long straight stretch from the shore inland. Mr. Hall, an engineer by trade, also planned the eastern edge of the park, the narrow wedge called the Panhandle, where today taller trees give away the age (and shelter) of this end of the park.

The remainder of the park is John McLaren's. His zest for bringing in plants from every corner of the world can be seen today in every meadow and in each long vista. The heartbreaking early failures—and there were many—are well documented in his own gardening book, written in 1908, *Gardening in California, Landscape and Flower*. In his words:

> The sand dunes of San Francisco... bordering on the Pacific Ocean, lie entirely open and exposed to the storms of winter... how to tie this moving mass of sand and to hold and bind it from drifting was the first problem to be solved by the park builders. The first experiment tried was sowing barley-seed thickly over the entire area... the seed sprouted and grew several inches, covering the sand for a few months, but it failed to hold the sands together after July, and the winds of August started (the dunes) moving again.
>
> The next attempt was... the Yellow Lupine (*Lupinus arboreus*), a strong-growing, perennial shrub which is a native of this section. The seeds were collected and broadcast... but this proved successful only in the better protected parts of the district.
>
> The Sea Bent Grass (*Ammophila arenaria*), a native of the maritime countries of Europe and successfully used in nearly all the coast countries of that continent, was next experimented with. This plant had been used in Denmark, perhaps more than in any other country, but France, Holland, Italy, Spain and also Great Britain had reclaimed many thousands of acres by means of this wonderful sand-binder.

GOLDEN
GATE
PARK

*A Scotsman
Tames the
Dunes*

The dune grass finally held, after seedlings survived two years in the nursery and another, tougher, test in the open. Once the advancing sand slowed, Mr. McLaren turned his attention to ornamental trees and shrubs, the front-line windbreak that made the remainder of the park possible. Establishing a windbreak proved as difficult as stopping the sand storms:

> A great many different species of trees were experimented with, including those especially suggested by European foresters, such as the Norway Maple, Sycamore, Maritime Pine, English Yew, Austrian Pine, and Elder and many others highly recommended. In exposed situations all of these, with the exception of the Maritime Pine, failed entirely.
> At the same time, many of our native trees and shrubs, including Monterey Cypress, Monterey Pine, Yellow Pine as well as Alders and Maples were set out. The Cottonwood, Scrub Oak, and other varieties of Oaks, were also given a trial, but, excepting the Monterey Cypress and Monterey Pine, all of them, like the hardier of the European introductions, did fairly well in the sheltered hollows only, where good soil and plenty of water were provided, while the Monterey Cypress and Monterey Pine alone stood the test of braving the storms and the blasting influence of the summer winds in the more exposed places and the district close to the shore.

The park unfolded before the eyes of a generation of San Franciscans; so successful were those early efforts that today, few schoolchildren know that the park was once a desert of lifeless sand dunes. Even cabdrivers tell visitors that the park has always been there—a compliment and yet a disservice to Messrs. Hall, McLaren and gardeners.

Past history would be just that, if the park today didn't live up to its miraculous beginnings. Golden Gate Park is so well regarded by San Franciscans, and so beautifully maintained for a municipal park, that the early high standards continue to this day. The financial support—the amount of money San Franciscans are willing to pay for not only Golden Gate Park, but most of the neighborhood parks as well—is the envy of urban park directors across North America. The staff of 99 gardeners is well above the complement for similar parks in the States; the park mirrors the city's pride of place.

Golden Gate Park was well used in 1895, as it is today. Here, families picnic at the Children's Playground, in the warmer east end of the park. (Courtesy Strybing Arboretum Society)

S. F. 405.   A Midwinter Day at Children's Playground, Golden Gate Park, San Francisco, Cal.

It is when the chains go up, the cars detoured, the roller skates and skateboards oiled, each Sunday morning at dawn, when San Franciscans head for Golden Gate Park to taste the freedom of the park without automobiles. For only a few hours each week, on Sundays, the eastern half of John F. Kennedy Drive becomes, all at once and on the same roadway, a pedestrian promenade, a bicycle path, a runway for runaway skateboards and skaters.

The road closure, like the controversial purchase of the parkland itself, was a wise political decision, allowing the real park supporters time to steal some time in their park. Without the intimate Sunday visits, or the responsive elected officials—then, as now—the park might not have shaped San Francisco, in temper and on paper. And without John McLaren's vision, horticultural skill, and determination, not only would the Rhododendron Dell be without its statue, the rhododendrons might not even be there at all. Mr. McLaren assured his immortality by first planting his beloved trees and shrubs, and then by setting the high standards of garden-making which future San Francisco gardeners were to follow.

Windmill Garden and Anglers Lodge

Stabilizing the dunes continues to this day, although the pioneering efforts of Mr. McLaren make today's barrier-making a much easier task; evidence of the shifting sands, and the grass planting, is everywhere evident along the Pacific shore of Golden Gate Park. Sprinklers have replaced the hand-watering of a century ago when gardeners carefully hand-brushed the packed sand way, every morning, from newly-planted specimens.

Near the dunes, on the western shore, the Dutch Windmill is another reminder of early park days when water and wind worked together to establish man-made meadows and shrub borders inland. The relic was recently restored, at great expense, making this touch of Holland—with its spectacular spring bulb display—one of the finest, and newest, park attractions. The Queen Wilhelmina Garden is further distinguished by its formal layout in the midst of informal, picturesque parkland.

The tall hedges marking the eastern boundary of the Dutch garden are particularly noteworthy; the mixed planting of pittosporum, myoperum and mirror plant (*Coprosma*) not only blend easily with one another but are reliably tough and hardy so close to the sea. Curiously, these hedges, and the hebes nearby, are all New Zealand and Australian natives, adapting easily to their new coastal conditions while protecting bulbs from Holland in the spring, and enclosing colorful borders later in the year.

In autumn, the sunken Queen Wilhelmina garden—which is remarkably warm thanks to sheltering from prevailing westerly winds off the sea, across the street—displays vivid chrysanthemums, and the last of the impatiens and petunias. In the shadow of the giant windmill, this pocket of warmth and bright color is always a pleasurable retreat, with its flower beds curving through and around the recessed lawn. Together, the flowers and old wooden park benches invite the city dweller to stop for a moment.

A mile inland, past acres of towering trees planted to break the wind, a little-known lodge rests within a pine grove, surrounded by two acres of plants—including early park introductions of acacia, *Leptospermum* and eucalyptus. Fisherman come from miles around to practice casting in the three huge pools stretching in front of the rustic lodge.

As gardening "beats" in Golden Gate Park go, the Anglers Lodge—with its comfortable fireplace inside, and handsome wood carving inside and out—is a most rewarding assignment. For years, it was the domain of Arnold Ward, a diplomat and gracious gardener who would interrupt his pruning on a moment's notice to talk about "his" fishing lodge garden which was, and is, "as pretty as you please". His penchant for carefully clipping each bush into shapes suiting his taste is still evident, but the new gardeners plan a less formal effect to the lodge garden.

The approach to the fishing lodge, off outer John F. Kennedy (North) Drive across from the Buffalo Paddock, is the first clue to its special place in the park. Remote and mysterious at first glimpse, yet intimate upon closer view, the lodge is half hidden by a mature Portugal Laurel (*Prunus lusitanica*) hedge, by rows of rhododendrons, recently renewed, and by 4-ft. hedges of the delicately-scented Mexican Orange (*Choisya ternata*) and the reliable *Hebe 'Menziesii'* curving up the gentle slope alongside the walkway.

Backed by taller hedges of copper-tinted eugenia, and scattered specimens of similarly-colored photinia, the stone path leads to the stone and wood lodge. On closer view, the lodge is immediately surrounded by more hedging—this one, the gardener's particular favorite, the aromatic California Bay Laurel (*Umbellularia californica*), a "pleasure" to prune.

The north entry gives way to the sunny southern exposure, where the gray, stone retaining wall and terrace warms weary fisherman and tender plants alike. A yellow-blooming Italian Jasmine climbs a trellis near a bed of yellow daffodils, on the knoll above the lawn sloping down to the casting pools.

Beside the water, layers of informal hedging—all subdued in color to harmonize with the country setting—separate the recessed pools from the hill above. Here, maroon-hued Hop Bush (*Dodonaea viscosa* 'Purpurea') is casually interspersed with Australian and New Zealand Tea Tree (*Leptospermum*) varieties. Fast-growing myoporum and rhamnus fill in behind and around the other plants, while accents of bright white daisies repeat the color splashes—nearly year-round—of the hebe and choisya on the north side of the lodge.

Opposite. The Dutch Windmill, recently restored, shelters a sunken bulb and flower garden, on a bed of grass, surrounded by hardy hedges close to the sea.

The Queen Wilhelmina Tulip Garden, here in its prime the last week of March.

Scented California Bay hedges—a "pleasure to prune"—anchor the entrance to the Anglers Lodge east of the windmill garden.

Choisya and hebe hedges partially hide the entrance to the Anglers Lodge.

Marguerites and New Zealand Tea trees color the west pathway in winter and reflect their flowers in the fly casting pools.

As with any garden, the Anglers Lodge garden changed with its new caretaker, Joe Giammattei, a native San Franciscan who rarely visited this part of this park in his youth. He continues to fight the invasion of the German Ivy, just as his predecessor did, but plans to introduce more deciduous trees to add an autumn spark of color beyond the dark brown building and under the evergreen canopy of pines. The weeping eucalyptus, everpresent in this end of the park, will assume a lesser role in the overall treescape.

The fishermen who use this retreat on public property know their good fortune so contribute substantially to its upkeep, thus providing a most sylvan setting for others. The casual visitor is encouraged to find a sunny spot to watch the fly casters while taking in the plantings and sea air. After several visits, many find this special spot irresistable, and minimum membership in the fisherman's club seems a necessity, if only to help preserve the historic park planting surrounding the lodge.

Out of view, but within a mile, are the only natural lakes in the park; the others are man-made. The Chain of Lakes stretches the width of the park, from north to south, and provided an opportunity for John McLaren to experiment with plants at home in bogs and ponds. The moody lakes, in shadow of shrubs and trees, make a striking contrast to the open and inviting Spreckles Lake, the model boating enthusiasts' landmark at the western end of the park.

Tall rhododendrons reach for light under open branches of Monterey Pine, Monterey Cypress and Eucalyptus, and therein lies the vestige of John McLaren's selection of plants. The eucalyptus, however, proved far more vigorous than planned and have crowded out many of the pine and cypress. Originally, the eucalyptus were imported to protect the pine and cypress seedlings, but the tenacious Australian trees soon took over from the California natives.

The western end of the park, with fewer buildings and people than the eastern portion, is a better showcase for less formal park plantings, is a windbreak and is the reason why any plants grew in the eastern half at all. Here too, as in the Presidio, tall trees reaching the end of their life cycle need replacement; this time the tree planting will be spread out over decades, rather than planted all at once, as was necessary in the early park history.

A spring scene near one of the Golden Gate Park meadows carved from the sand dunes.

Shrubs and trees along the perimeter of the park camouflage the city beyond; in keeping with the original plan and providing today an instant change of scene for those entering the park. White-washed stucco houses end abruptly at the evergreen park, as do most of the high-speed roads so disliked by John McLaren. Even Sunset Boulevard—the city's handsome tree-lined thoroughfare—disappears into the greenery at its southern (36th Avenue) entry into the park, confusing many a motorist, but pleasing park planners and preservationists alike.

Only one high-speed road cuts straight through the park from north to south, its placement permanently dividing the park into two distinct places: the man-made wilderness to the west; the tour buses, tea garden, glasshouses and museums to the east.

The eastern half of the park is intensely used and gardened. The ever-popular Japanese Tea Garden draws busloads of visitors but San Franciscans have memorized which hours and days the tea garden is open, quiet, and without charge. The Strybing Arboretum, across the roadway, is a plant-enthusiast's outdoor classroom, while classes of schoolchildren find the fossils and indoor specimens at the Academy of Sciences far more interesting. The magnificent glass Conservatory houses a tropical collection of plants, and in the valley carved below the Conservatory, massed flowers and fascinating floral plaques spell out welcome and other messages to all passers-by.

To see this end of Golden Gate Park on a Sunday morning, when the main drive is closed to through automobile traffic, is to experience the park as even John McLaren would not have anticipated. The mass of humanity, tolerating one another and quietly absorbing the surrounding beauty, listening to the music from the bandstand or bicycle tires skimming over smooth pavement, is a sight and sound unequaled mid-week in the park.

The Japanese Tea Garden, renowned for its cherry blossom show at the end of March, is equally vivid in autumn, when the trees turn color and the form takes shape. Here, on November 13, the trees still hold their leaves, indicating the long slow seasonal changes in the maritime exposure.

The eastern end of the park has almost as many individual support groups as blades of grass, and this, too, contributes to the enormous popularity of the park. The Strybing Arboretum Society has a loyal band of volunteer tour guides and horticulturists, Rose Society members eagerly prune the bushes in the Rose Garden each winter, the newly-formed Conservatory Friends support, financially, the enormous glass house and its collection, the San Francisco Lawn Bowling Club, established in 1901, keeps an eye on the greens, and other specialized supporters keep an eye on other parts of their beloved park.

Tea Garden,
Arboretum
and
Manicured Beds

Watching over the entire park is another group, Friends of Recreation and Parks, whose generosity takes pressure off the (always inadequate) municipal park budget. The museums—art and science—face one another across the sunken bandstand garden, and each, through its membership, supports park endeavors, although the debate still rages over whether museums and parks are compatible in the first place.

The deYoung Museum is a relic from the 1894 Mid-Winter Fair, and shelters a most beguiling outdoor cafe garden, with trellis work and seasonal flowers, in a courtyard behind the museum. A pond and appropriate bog plants graces the entrance to the art museum, while, across the way, the California Academy of Sciences stands in the shadow of the Shakespeare Garden, established in the 1920s by, among others, the Academy's Curator of Botany, Alice Eastwood.

The Japanese Tea Garden is the main feature, particularly in cherry blossom season at the end of March. Fall is delightful here as well, as evergreen pines and cypress shelter deciduous trees which make a remarkable fall display before shedding their leaves. The tea garden often surprises visitors looking for a broad sweep of lawn, as at the University of Washington's Japanese Tea Garden, or the expansive, open Japanese Garden on display at the Missouri Botanical Gardens. San Francisco's tea garden is really not so much a garden as an entire village in miniature.

Designed, in fact, as a Japanese village for the 1894 Mid-Winter Fair held in Golden Gate Park, the tiny Japanese Tea Garden is a relic from a century ago when the park was new and the Fair needed a draw. Moon bridges and stone steps slowly lead the visitor through the Lilliputian stroll garden, compact and mysterious at every turn. Glimpses of the tiered temple—a remnant of the 1915 world's fair— surrounded by manicured Plume Cedar (*Cryptomeria japonica*) entice the stroller onward, while the tea house provides a refreshing pause before continuing past the waterfalls to the Zen garden beyond.

Pruning is the specialty in the Japanese Tea Garden and is developed to a high art form by the staff of three gardeners year-round. Some trees take three days of a gardener's time to prune while ohers require outside help to cut and shape to perfection. The shaping process can be as fascinating as the stroll through the village. One side is shaped, then the other pruned to match; finally, the tree is thinned, but not opened up too much—a delicate operation, performed at least once a year on most specimens.

The Hagiwara family tended the garden, for the city, for generations until the second World War, when the garden was abandoned and renamed The Oriental Garden. Brought back after the war to its earlier perfection, the garden is viewed by 2,000 to 5,000 people a day.

Wild strawberries once covered **Strawberry Hill,** the highest vantage point in the park, now obscured by mature second-growth trees camouflaging the hilltop. Most of the native trees were cut for firewood either before the 1906 earthquake or immediately after. The hill, centrally located in the park, served the water needs of the park from a reservoir and so defined the bounds which park planners followed for years. The hill is surrounded by **Stow Lake**—one of the several man-made lakes in the park.

The 70-acre **Strybing Arboretum,** established by bequest of Helene Strybing in the 1930s, contains a wide variety of plants from around the world, but specializes in those plants from temperate climates similar to that of San Francisco. The coast redwood trail is popular for viewing not only the tall, handsome California natives but for shade-loving groundcovers which thrive beneath the *Sequoia sempervirens.* The Fragrance Garden is full of perfume year-round while the Sunset Demonstration Garden, within the arboretum, shows vines and groundcovers at their peak and in their decline, making choices easier for home gardeners wanting to try those plants on display.

The indoor workshops, lectures, and the **Helen Crocker Russell Horticultural Library** at Strybing draw as many visitors as does the garden itself, and provides essential horticultural background for novice and advanced gardeners alike.

Strybing's annual spring plant sale is the highlight of the gardening year for San Francisco gardeners. The line of gardeners forms around the building to buy one-of-a-kind plants nurtured by volunteers and nursery staff in anticipation of the big yearly sale. Many of the exotic plants found in city gardens trace their beginnings to the annual Strybing sale, and to smaller Strybing sales held in the courtyard throughout the year. The sale is one of the few chances to pick up plants seen and admired in the park.

Only the most tender plants are grown in the **Conservatory,** as in most municipal glasshouses, but the Golden Gate Park Conservatory, in recent years, began to collect coolhouse orchids, particularly Masdevallias from South America. Behind the public greenhouse, rows of orchids line the hidden but equally interesting greenhouses.

Gigantic tropical plants reach for the sky in the central dome of the building, which is the oldest in the park. Pockets of rare tropicals surround the more familiar philodendrons and ferns, and the orchid

The west wing of the Conservatory, pictured here, encloses splendid holiday flower displays, while the central dome shelters tall tropicals and a fine orchid show. The warm, humid, east wing houses a lily pond and more exotics, while the greenhouses behind the main building cover collections yet to come on view. To keep the collections at a comfortable temperature, a fogger machine is used, essential for greenhouse success even in foggy San Francisco.

case displays showy specimens during peak bloom. In the east wing, the lily pond supports minute water life and plants, the most famous being the Victoria Waterlily, while the west wing is a seasonal showcase, winter, spring, summer and fall.

Floral Plaques made with low-growing plants—2,500 in some designs—hug the ground on either side of the Conservatory entrance and spell out messages of greeting on the hillside. The changing of the plaques, like the changing of the guard in London, is a San Francisco event, and a gardening assignment requiring much patience. The entire operation must be performed, days on end, on hands and knees, while explaining, over and over, the difference between Irish Moss and Scotch Moss to visitors supervising the four-day changeover.

On the valley floor, 13,000 square feet of geometric patterns outline beds of seasonal flowers, an extravagance that San Franciscans have come to expect each season. The park nursery, within its eight acres, supplies 240,000 annual bedding plants, twice a year, to fill the parterres, which remain in place four months each. The planting patterns change from year to year, so that a sweep of narcissus may only reappear several years later.

The rhododendrons in the **Rhododendron Dell,** the **fuchsias** and **camellias** and **roses** all set aside in gardens of their own, serve specialized interests in this much-visited end of the park. The fall **dahlia** display, on the lee side of the Conservatory, results from the hard work of one dedicated, volunteer gardener who has a special interest in the dahlia—the official San Francisco city flower.

The pollarded plane trees, so full in summer and shorn in winter, give character and depth to the sunken **Bandstand Garden,** where opera and music fill the summer air. As the music filters into the **Shakespeare Garden** nearby, one can easily feel transported back to another slower time, when laurel and holly graced old gardens, when drama and opera set a magical stage in everyday life.

Floral plaques are filled with low, slow-growing plants and changed twice a year.

Conservatory Valley, ablaze with daffodils in February, provides shelter for sunbathers and bookworms on a warm winter day.

The Dahlia Garden, east of the Conservatory, reaches its prime in autumn. Dahlia grower Roy Takeuchi established this garden which celebrates San Francisco's official city flower.

The bust of Shakespeare, enclosed behind glass, in the Shakespeare Garden behind the Academy of Sciences. Carved plaques hold flower quotations from the bard's pen.

Unaltered by time and southeast of the Conservatory, is the discreet **Bowling Green**—actually three greens, covering two acres—and handsome enclosures of olive, escallonia and pittosporum hedges sheltering the players in their starched whites. John McLaren was a Lawn Bowls enthusiast which explains why this corner of the park is devoted to this old-fashioned game.

Gardening in this enclave has special requirements—the lawns are cut daily to ⅛ inch by an Australian machine which is almost as old-fashioned as the game itself. The lumbering, awkward "30-inch Queen," as the cutter is called, shears off the grass tips, then gardeners must keep constant watch for fungus diseases ready to attach the closely-cropped bent grass. Once a year, very sharp sand—not the ordinary San Francisco kind—is worked into the soil beneath the greens to offset compacting which comes from constant gamesplaying.

Tall, graceful, tree ferns grow in groves nearby. An 1899 bequest from the Jose De Laveaga estate was the impetus for the original grove, between the bowling green and the Conservatory. The first ferns came from a generous New Zealander, who, after visiting the park and talking with John McLaren, went home and shipped a "box of tree ferns, entirely without cost to us," Mr. McLaren told Alice Eastwood in 1932. The De Lavaega Dell today is on the site of the former Deer Park; the deer and elk were moved to make way for the stately tree ferns from New Zealand.

The park is well used, which some say, is the mark of its success. Parks cannot·be overused, but they fall from underuse, in the view of landscape architect Kal Platt, whose firm, SWA Group, has designed many San Francisco parks and squares. The formula for park success combines people and design. The SWA-designed Sydney Walton Square, on the northern edge of the Financial District, for example, is packed with office workers mid-day, just as Golden Gate Park is filled each day of the week—people, particularly San Franciscans, enjoy watching one another as well as watching the grass grow.

Golden Gate Park owes its initial success to the extraordinary plantsmen whose ideals and ideas shaped the three miles of meadow and wood and flower beds so heavily used by San Franciscans today.

A sporting game—Lawn Bowls—on a closely manicured green, is played today as it was at the turn of the century, when John McLaren carved the greens in his park. Olive and pittosporum hedges shelter flowers and players in this warm eastern pocket of the park.

Heavy and clumsy, this cutting machine, affectionately called "The 30 inch Queen" in its native Australia, keeps the bowling greens clipped within an eighth of an inch above ground. These game lawns are cut daily.

Any San Franciscan, if asked which garden in the city is the most visited and photographed, will answer, without hesitation, The Japanese Tea Garden in Golden Gate Park. The Crookedest Street in the World (not really) on Russian Hill might take second place, with its impressive hydrangea show in summer.

Not unlike native New Yorkers who have yet to visit their Statue of Liberty, or native Londoners, Buckingham Palace, San Franciscans leave one of their finest gardens for the tourists. The tour operators are a step ahead of the natives, who hardly know that a magnificent seaside garden anchors the south tower of the Golden Gate Bridge.

To be sure, San Franciscans show visitors the famous bridge, but from the paved-over north tower lookout, with its honky-tonk, flowerless environs framing the familiar city skyline view. Meanwhile, tourists by the busload photograph one another beside the south tower's splendid flower display set against the backdrop of the bridge across San Francisco Bay.

The south tower garden is a study in seaside hardiness, wind resistance and Mediterranean plant influence all on less than five acres. One of the country's best demonstration seaside gardens, and the best public perennial garden outside of Golden Gate Park, each compartment offers serious strollers a lesson in which plants suit the mild San Francisco climate best, which hedges hold back the sea breezes, which native plants thrive on neglect in remote outposts.

As with any garden, public or private, one gardener created the mood and image for others to enjoy. Just as the bridge itself was one man's engineering masterpiece, the south tower garden is one man's horticultural dream, quietly executed. Golden Gate Bridge head gardener Tom Edwards gives credit to his predecessor Hugh Wallace, who envisioned the garden in the 1950s, but it is Mr. Edwards who has, for the past decade, modified and molded the garden into a horticultural showpiece. He has, for example, replaced extensive, labor-intensive beds of annuals with more permanent perennials, and filled the hillside and rock gardens with an astonishing variety of year-round blooms. Unlike many public gardens today, the bridge garden hardly relies on instant color of bedded annuals, changed two or three times yearly.

A small patch of lawn offsets the statue of Bridge engineer Joseph Strauss at the garden entrance. To the right of the lawn, triple hedging frames the bridge and bay view, while protecting visitors from stiff westerly breezes. The graceful evergreen *Cotoneaster parneyi (C. lacteus)*, which displays an abundance of

THE
GOLDEN GATE
BRIDGE
GARDEN

*Tourists'
Favorite*

The south tower of the Golden Gate Bridge looms over the colorful garden so photographed by visitors to the city. Santolina edges central flower border, triple hedging borders the main pathway beyond. (Henry Bowles photograph)

white flowers in spring, and red berries in winter, shelters the smaller hedges of *Cistus* 'Doris Hibberson' and another of lavender cotton, *Santolina chamaecyparissus*, kept constantly clipped to retain perfect form.

Beyond the lawn and opposite the triple hedgerow, a hillside of flowers frames the bridge offering yet another splendid view. The horticultural skill needed to keep the steep hillside in bloom is, to some, almost as impressive as the engineering skill used in the bridge beyond. Allowed to wander freely on the slope, Mexican Evening Primrose (*Oenethera berlandieri*) blankets the upper reaches with profuse pale pink blooms all summer long, and shows just how hardy the evening primrose family is under the toughest of conditions. Below the pink flowers, another Mexican plant, the Mexican Bush Sage (*Salvia leucantha*) sends up tall velvety spikes alongside impressive, deep blue spires of Pride of Madeira (*Echium fastuosum*).

Other rugged but handsome additions include hebes from New Zealand, Pincushion (*Leucospermum*) from South Africa, California poppies, morning glories (*Ipomea spp.*) which have spread from 2 or 3 original plants, and clusters of Society Garlic (*Tulbaghia violacea*). Two of Mr. Edwards' experiments—the "showoff" Honey Bush (*Melianthus major*) and the old-fashioned Jerusalem Sage (*Phlomis fruticosa*)—proved as reliable as nearby hillside neighbors.

An uphill path leads visitors past a free-form rock garden, carved from an uncompromising site, and harboring tiny specimens of *Geranium incanum*, California Poppies ("That's the flower I'm asked about more than any other," Mr. Edwards opines), allysum, heuchera, dianthus, *Saponaria ocymoides* and other wedged-in plants clearly enjoying the confines. Below are edgings of familiar flowers, including lobelias in both deep blue and pale blue, a particular color combination favored by Mr. Edwards.

The blue agapanthus is a favorite San Francisco flower, adapting well to seaside conditions. The hillside is filled with perennials, and some annuals, that thrive in the wind and fog; the California poppy is the most sought-after, and asked about, flower at the Golden Gate Bridge garden. (Henry Bowles photograph)

Fog blankets the garden, some days, but the tourists visit in any weather. Gardeners Tom Edwards and Diane Schaumleffel, left, tend the low santolina hedge while visitors search for a camera angle near the hidden bridge.

The bridge tower barely visible, upper photo, under a cover of fog in late May. Flower colors brighten the scene on foggy days.

Exotics steal the spotlight, temporarily, beneath the south tower of the Golden Gate Bridge. Here, Pride of Madeira (*Echium fastuosum*) sends up early summer spires, highlighting the range of flowers possible by the sea.

A downhill path appears to end at the foot of the hillside garden, but a short excursion beyond the fence brings a wildflower-strewn slope into clear view, exposing the splendour of the bridge underpinnings and the abandoned military outpost, Fort Point, on the bluff beneath the bridge. Alongside this precipitous path, native and escaped flowers share the promontory offering a microcosmic view of the fine natural setting that existed before waves of settlers arrived.

The manicured garden above stands in contrast to the more natural, but unkempt, point of land between the garden and the bridge underpinnings. Most of the short-term, hurried visitors obviously prefer Mr. Edwards' man-made garden to the wilder hillside below. Judging from the daily onslaught of out-of-towners, more photographs of this garden exist in scrapbooks worldwide than perhaps of any other landmark in San Francisco. The ironies are these: the bridge garden was created for visitors and San Franciscans, yet few San Franciscans have discovered the fine demonstration garden in their midst; and the enormous variety of plants and flowers is often wasted on the busloads of tourists, intent on keeping a schedule and clicking a camera.

Mr. Edwards, with a crew of only four, and an unheated, unlighted greenhouse, has enthusiastically perservered and created a grand seaside habitat, unawed by the Golden Gate Bridge towering above the flowers. In the spirit of a true gardener, Mr. Edwards smiles as he sums up his priorities: "I'd like to think that the bridge is more beautiful because of this garden."

THE FILBERT STREET STEPS

Secret Telegraph Hill Oasis

San Francisco's relentless, north to south, east to west, grid with only the central hills to break the pattern, looks handsome on paper, and many a visitor has been fooled into thinking those streets really exist. In actual practice, the streets stop and start, climb precipitously, then, in steep descent, frighten the uninitiated. The steepest of the streets take no automobiles at all, and few motorists would try the harrowing inclines.

Telegraph Hill is criss-crossed with alleys and streets that go nowhere, a walker's hill above the warm eastern shore, where early settlers put up wooden cottages, then saved their home with home-made wine, stashed in cellars, during the 1906 fire. Telegraph Hill's character is largely attributable to its characters; the Filbert Street Steps is no exception.

Filbert Street appears on every city map, heading straight west, for Russian Hill, from its humble origins on the lee side of Telegraph Hill. It hardly goes a quarter mile before wooden steps replace the paved street. Alongside the steep, wooden staircase lies a lush green garden that, as it climbs toward the top of the hill, transports the visitor from the real world to the imagined, from the Financial District into what might be a Hollywood movie set for the 1937 movie, *Lost Horizon.*

The public garden to the left, the private gardens, along the right, on the Filbert Street Steps, two steep stairways beneath Coit Tower. Campanula and fuchsias spill over the wood staircase.

Napier Lane, a wood-planked 'street' adjoining the Filbert Street Steps, carpeted in campanula, iris, fuchsias and roses in May. Gardner Gary Kray and Filbert Street Steps garden at the end of Napier Lane in the photo.

On the Greenwich Street Steps, below Montgomery Street, the gardens are less visited but no less inviting. Here, May flowers outside one of the cottages along the steps.

A close view of Napier Lane gardens, with contented cat holding down the fence. The stairway gardens are on the lee side of Telegraph Hill, protected from wind but shaded in afternoons.

A garden along the Filbert Street steps, on Telegraph Hill.

Indeed, the two characters who shaped the hill where Hollywood beauty queens from the silent movie era, both of whom retired to San Francisco. Grace Marchant, a Hollywood stuntwoman, laid out the Filbert Street steps, and her daughter, an RKO chorus girl, worked her magic on the adjoining Greenwich Street Steps. Their flair, their sense of beauty, is shared at every turn.

Yet both hillside gardens are captives of their immediate surroundings. The Greenwich Street Steps are more open to bay views, being the last street before the cliff falls off toward the Bay, yet the shrubbery obscures the northern shoreline from permanent view. The homes climb the hill to the south of the garden, standing between the garden and the sun. Shade-loving plants thrive here; and the spring-flowering trees, planted in the sunniest corner, are a spectacular sight. Baby Tear piles up around delicate paths, and bulbs surprise at each season.

The lower Greenwich Street Steps are now paved with a hard surface, removing a touch of charm still enjoyed on the Filbert Street Steps. Wooden planking still stands along the lower Filbert Street Steps garden and into the tiny alleys that fan out from the steps. Napier Lane and its garden is every bit as beguiling as the long stairway garden along Filbert Street.

Adding to the allure of both gardens are the wooden cottages and billowing gardens flowing out of garden gates along the lanes. Private and public effort work well together here, giving a cohesion missing in even the best of the rest.

The Filbert Street Steps—the garden of Grace Marchant fame, and now officially named in her honor—fall down the hillside east of Montgomery Street, where streets are narrow and parking simply doesn't exist. She started the garden when she was 63 years old and for 30 years held court for anyone who admired her handiwork. She and her gardens became legends together.

The stairway leading to Coit Tower on the Upper Filbert Street Steps. Private gardens spill over on to the public stairway.

The carpet of Baby Tear tolerates the summer sun, but needs winter moisture and shade to survive along the Filbert Street Steps. Roses and Datura and fuchsia provide added summer interest behind the wooden gate leading to the stairway gardens.

The seasons come and go with the sun, rather than with the snow and heat. The sun disappears behind the hill in November to reemerge in March, slowly working its way from the stairway to the hillocks on the south and east. A wooden gate defines the entry to the acre of roses and datura, raspberry, fuchsias and more roses. 'Tropicana' and 'Royal Sunset', both bold in color, were her favorite roses, and gardener Gary Kray, who now maintains the garden to high standard, keeps those roses in her memory.

The 'Royal Sunset' rose is fleeting, in bud one day and gone the next, but the 'Tropicana' lasts for days, even, on Telegraph Hill. Old-fashioned park benches are well placed and half-hidden behind the shrubbery within the wooden gate garden, so that gardeners—or movie directors?—might sit and watch the roses perform.

The upper Filbert and Greenwich Street gardens—above and west of Montgomery Street—are equally alluring, and less known to San Franciscans than to tourists visiting Colt Tower just above the gardens. The private gardens spill out and over the paved steps and the berries in winter and acacias in spring hover over the lanes and give them its character. Hydrangea hedges and bougainvillea thrive here, while nandina and camellias brighten the winter scape on the steep hill.

Old wooden benches, painted red, rest on a landing by the upper Filbert Street Steps, offering a fine view of the Bay Bridge and Berkeley to the east. In a walker's city, these four stairways, side by side, spilling down the east face of Telegraph Hill, are without equal as gardening showcase—a gift to the city from Grace Marchant, her daughter, Gary Kray, and all the other splendid gardeners who live and garden along the lanes.

Hypericum flowers flourish in May along the steep Filbert Street Steps above Montgomery. Gardeners who live along the steps care for the gardens there.

This red-painted wood bench awaits weary climbers on the Upper Filbert Street Steps, directly below Coit Tower. View east, with San Francisco Bay in distance.

In winter, nandina berries combine with red camellias behind the long bench, left, on the Upper Filbert Street Steps on Telegraph Hill.

82

Tilling Together

If sharing an autumn banquet with dinner partners from a group called SLUG dulls one's appetite, an explanation is in order.

SLUG is to San Francisco what BUG is to Boston, DUG is to Denver, and Philadelphia Green is to the founding city of this city green movement. An estimated 2,000 eager San Francisco gardeners join their counterparts nationwide in cultivating, preserving and protecting minuscule to grand urban plots, reclaiming 'paper' streets that might otherwise lie fallow, or worse, degenerate into rubbish heaps or paved parking lots.

Not all of the city's 2,000 community gardeners attend SLUG's November harvest banquet, but the fruits of their year-round labors are shared and compared quite favorably with the finest catered affair downtown. Freshly picked lettuce leaves make their way into salads and centerpieces, local honey is recognized immediately ("Hmmm, isn't this *fennel* honey from that garden in the Mission?"), and all is washed down with California wine before homemade apple pie appears.

Community gardening is in its infancy in San Francisco. East Coast cities have had such programs in place for years and claim many more than the 60 plots presently cultivated in San Francisco. A national organization, the American Community Garden Association (ACGA), brings the older and newer city establishments together for advice and meetings.

The typical SLUG gardener, surprisingly, is not always an apartment-dweller with little outdoor gardening space, although quite a number fall into this category. Others may have gardens of their own—in the shade—so search for sunny sites to grow their crops or cut flowers. A third category is made up of gardeners well along in years whose "reason for waking up in the morning" is the shared pleasures of comraderie and the cultivation of their plots.

Still others join to try gardening under glass or lath. It is no coincidence that the Fort Mason Community Garden, with its tidy greenhouse, lathhouse and superb location by the bay just downwind from the Golden Gate Bridge foghorns, is one of the most sought-after gardens in the city; in fact the waiting list for the 113 over-sized plots is two years. Tourists flock to Fisherman's Wharf directly below historic Fort Mason, unaware of this serene park and community garden just a few steep steps up a shaded stairway across from Aquatic Park. Younger foreign tourists have, however, already discovered the Youth Hostel on the hill overlooking this garden, so gardening advice often comes in several languages, as youths share their enthusiasm with native San Franciscans. In park planner jargon, this "mixed use" is a model of efficient land-use as well as international good will.

The remaining 59 community gardens are farther from the tourist's eye, but no less green and inviting. School yards, street rights-of-way and patches of parkland last year produced $350,000 worth of vegetable crops and saved the city's maintenance crews $1,000 for each clean-up call not made because such vacant spaces were being tended. Many of the gardens produce year around; up to four different crops can be coaxed out of one 20 square foot plot, using "French Intensive" and other growing methods.

Novice gardeners learn which cover crops (clovers, fava beans, and others) add the most nutrition to their soil, when to turn such crops under, and how long to leave them between plantings in this year-round maritime climate. SLUG teaches techniques necessary for crop success just as the Strybing Arboretum Society in Golden Gate Park teaches ornamental gardening to devoted horticulturalists. SLUG and Strybing together have turned out many of this city's keen gardeners, and led them on the path to the California Horticultural Society and other rarified gardening associations. But in SLUG circles, it's quite debatable whether the individual gardener or the city is the true beneficiary of this vast gardening expertise.

Gardeners in these plots on the top of Potrero Hill have a fine view from their community garden looking west toward the summer fog on Twin Peaks. Where city streets meet hill tops, community gardens flourish.

In February, cover crops and seedlings blanket the small Community gardening plots, in demand year-round in San Francisco's maritime climate.

The lathhouse at Fort Mason Community Garden, with Youth Hostel on the hill beyond. Within sight and sound of the Golden Gate Bridge, this popular garden has a waiting list of two years.

Opposite. Cobbles are the stone of distinction in many San Francisco gardens, just as bluestone distinguishes Manhattan gardens, and brick, Boston. (Henry Bowles photograph)

IV.   THE PRIVATE GARDENS

*A
Child's Garden
on
Parnassus
Heights*

This beguiling January garden is singular proof that children, cities, and city gardens can indeed be synthesized into statements of beauty and frivolity. Here in the center of the San Francisco, on the east slope of Mt. Sutro, is a superb children's garden carved from a steep, uninhabitable hillside that rises precipitously three stories from the back entry. Every corner of this tiny tri-level city space—including thin air for the grand treehouse retreat—is used by the young and old(er) of this family.

A small lawn, a lofty perch, steps well placed and a staged wooden platform all demand attention simultaneously with the delicate sidelined flower beds that complement the whole. Space-saving vines climb fences while children climb rope ladders to the treehouse designed by father Bruce McDermott. Two mature trees—an evergreen pittosporum in the center, and a deciduous old plum on the upper slope—play important roles in making the family-planned compound an integral entity.

The soggy, sloping rock garden wedged against the house proved too formidable a task so the designer Charles Grimaldi was enlisted to create a floral bridge between the lower house interior and upper garden reaches. Mr. Grimaldi, in turn, unloaded his own backyard and favorite San Francisco plants into each carefully-placed alpine crevice. (Some garden designers prefer to work on paper, others prefer to dig in the soil and create along the way; this designer and family chose the latter approach).

From the living room window seats, only the exquisite rock garden and taller treehouse come into view. But from the upper story balcony, the central play area and wet winter lawn come into view.

Bruce and Lynn McDermott purchased their turn-of-the-century home 10 years ago and quickly realized that their back yard, like so many San Francisco lots, was unsuitable for small children. A typical view greeted the newlyweds: a bare, concrete, retaining wall the width of the back property line, holding the hillside from slipping downslope. The design solution came in three phases spanning several years. To level the central, hard clay slope meant back-breaking weekend work, but the children—both then under 5 years—soon had their patch of grass topped by a small swing set. The leveling project stopped "when we couldn't dig into the hill any further!"

A half year of planning preceded the treehouse construction. In order to save as much of the mature plum tree that stood in the upper garden, Mr. McDermott studied the limb structure for several months so that his final design would not damage the tree. His brainchild was fashioned up and around, not bulldozed through, the tree limbs. Father and son hammered together and the treehouse took shape over many weekends. Young Graham, now 7, has given his father's design a stamp of approval, with one minor reservation: "I think I'd like a second story someday." In winter, the sunlight filters through the bare branches, warming the children's hut and the primrose path beneath. But sunlight is fleeting between storms and then dappled, come February, when the pink plum blossoms arrive to announce San Francisco's early spring.

The rock garden is a showcase for the designer's favored plants, nurtured with care in Mr. Grimaldi's own garden until a client calls. In summer, the primroses give way to a lush carpet of lobelia, impatiens and alyssum spilling over and around the permanent collection of white French strawberry, ornamental grasses, ferns and dwarf evergreens.

Along the wooden, side yard boundaries, the pale pink, scented *Jasminum polyanthum* vine flourishes, as it does in so many San Francisco gardens; indeed it runs rampant if left unchecked. Shade-loving abutilons step up the hillside with Finger Ferns (which are allowed to remain), Lady Ferns (which are pulled up) and Sword Ferns (which tend to outgrow their confines). A thorny pyracantha towers above the fence line, providing privacy and a winter splash of white flowers seen from the bedroom balcony above.

The shallow steps of the primrose path lead to a space-saving, rope ladder. Alongside the treehouse entry and stretching the width of the lot is a second flower bed filled with hedging of the ever-reliable (for San Franciscans) New Zealand Hebe, and scented ginger and rosemary tucked in behind the 2 ft. high retaining wall. Along the back property line, behind the wooden platform, is another scented beauty, the *Magnolia grandiflora* 'St. Mary', which remains evergreen and small—a fine combination for any tree on compact city lots. Standard abutilons and privet (*Ligustrum japonicum* 'Texanum') serve by camouflaging the unattractive concrete wall. Descending the wooden platform, a curved flower bed harbors more gifts from Mr. Grimaldi's collection, including the year-round bloomer, Chinese Foxglove, *Rehmannia angulata*, and the South American herb, *Billbergia*. Climbing the wooden fence above is the shade-loving Firecracker Vine from Paraguay, *Manettia bicolor*, growing in concert with the dimunitive Cigar Plant from Mexico and Jamaica, *Cuphea ignea*.

A fine but unruly evergreen clematis vine (*Clematis armandii*) recently succumbed nearby, the victim of its own weight and wanderlust. This San Francisco standby once draped over the boundary line and everything else in its path as well; but needed more attention than the children which was its downfall. The children, in turn, give their undivided attention to only one plant in the garden: the evergreen tree towering above the rock garden that, from its Greek origins translates to 'pitch seed'. The children do just that—pitch the seeds—when the sticky *Pittosporum undulatum* capsules emerge after the scented spring flower display. With Firecracker Vines, and Cigar Plants, and Pitch Seed trees, a child's imagination takes flight; with primrose paths and attendant snails and slugs, Beauty and the Beast(s) is played out. And between the warm January rains, the children have their version of paradise just outside the back door. The spacious suburban lawn has clearly met its match.

The primrose path rises toward the retreat made of redwood. Bruce McDermott carved the treehouse around existing plum tree limbs and added a porch, right, for garden-viewing.

The view from the treehouse, showing the primrose path leading from lower rock garden. The treehouse entry is extra high, to allow grown-ups entry too.

January view from the master bedroom shows tri-level garden, with treehouse hidden, upper left. The rock garden, lower right, slopes toward the sunken living room windows, where the view is of year-round bloom.

NORTH →

87

*A Modern
Sculpture
Garden
Near the
Presidio*

On any wet, winter, January day in San Francisco, when hard city surfaces are beaten by the rains, this garden has a Roman goddess to soften the showers and soothe the spirit. In the process of redirecting the rains, the goddess has transformed a contemporary garden into a work of art, not unlike the fine sculpture gardens of ancient Greece and Rome. The Mediterranean influence—in plantings, in garden art, in sunlight off the bay—is strongly felt here by the sea, halfway around the globe.

Serenely and surely, the goddess, Egeria, reigns over this confined space. The 1,000-pound bronze nymph, carved by Greek sculptor Aristides Demetrios of San Francisco for Mr. and Mrs. Johnson S. Bogart, is a modern maiden, indeed. The sculpture is tall and lean, surrounded by water plants not yet discovered in the 7th Century B.C., when Egeria's myth held sway. The sculptured waterfall also succeeds in obscuring a modern annoyance unheard of centuries ago: shrill city noises, night and day.

This is not a typical 'before' and 'after' showpiece; the garden of these art patrons was quite satisfactory at the outset, which made the transformation even more difficult for the sculptor and his landscape collaborator. The Bogarts had lived through many seasons in the house and garden but wanted an artistic design approach, rather than a straightforward horticultural make-over. They achieved both in the process.

The house itself covers much of this corner lot, leaving a long rectangular paved surface parallel to the back of the house. Two house additions—a north kitchen wing and a south dining wing—protruded, side by side, into the back garden, with approximately 10 ft. between the two: just enough space for some shade-loving camellias with bare earth beneath. The view from both wings might have suggested placing a sculpture along the far wall, in direct line of sight from all back rooms. But the sculptor and his clients opted for the unusual: the goddess would occupy rather the tight space between the two wings, where her presence and waterfall could be sensed—and touched almost—at every turn indoors as well as out.

Choosing companion poolside plants proved almost as difficult as the art piece itself—how does a landscape architect upstage or downplay a goddess in his midst? Not only did Richard Schadt (who has collaborated with sculptor Demetrios for 16 years in San Francisco) need to know which plants would take the damp and deliberate splash, but the forms of each plant had to complement, not compete. In the northeast corner behind the sculpture, for example, the bold, strap-like leaves that looked so fine on paper jarred the senses on moving day. Lower, more rounded plant forms took their place.

In that corner, a magnificent Coral-bark Maple (*Acer palmatum* 'Senkaki') telegraphs its winter beauty. The dampness only deepens the red of the maple bark and bare branches. The form and color subtly complement Egeria.

In the pool itself, which is only a foot deep, two plants which prefer bog conditions thrive: the filmy, slender-stemmed sedge, *Cyperus isocladus,* and the distinctive rushlike horsetail, *Equisetum hyemale.* Both are contained in pots sunken underwater. The horsetail particularly needs restraint because of its invasive tendencies. The shallow depth of the pool does not permit fish to thrive.

Alongside the pool, planted in the amended sandy soil, massed azaleas (*Rhododendron* 'Fielder's White') create their own splash during late January bloom, while the tender Brazilian Yesterday-Today-and-Tomorrow shrub (*Brunsfelsia pauciflora calycina*) and the Heartleaf Bergenia (*Bergenia cordifolia*) await their turn for later bloom.

The Australian Bluebell Creeper (*Sollya heterophylla*) which climbs or creeps before putting out summer-long, brilliant blue bells, is combined with the summer blue of Dwarf Periwinkle (*Vinca minor*). For contrast, the stiffer-leaved groundcover *Cotoneaster dammeri* spills on the opposite side of the pool and displays its red fruit in the fall. The white and red of winter, then, give way to the blues of summer, followed by the cotoneaster red and maple-leaved yellow in autumn.

Two poolside shrubs, chosen for dependable glossy year-round foliage and fine form, are the Lily-of-the-valley Shrub (*Pieris japonica*) and the darker-leaved *Camellia sasanqua*. Both are used in many San Francisco gardens to provide essential background structure. Another shrub chosen for year-round reliability is the Sweet Box (*Sarcocca ruscifolia*) which is smaller than the others and produces unobtrusive but scented spring flowers, followed by red fruit.

The dramatic setting for the goddess and companion plants was made possible by one subtle change—moving the garden fence several feet toward the street, opening up the entire north end of the garden to more sunlight and circulation. Garden party guests circulate freely, and the sculpture doesn't loom or overwhelm, as it might in a more central spot in the garden.

Egeria was the mistress, adviser, and later wife, of the second king of Rome, Numa Pompilius. The myth held that she was so distraught over the king's death, she melted into tears. Diana turned Egeria into a fountain.

Thus, this thoroughly modern garden evokes the most ancient of city and civilized endeavors: the art of exquisite garden-making in crowded, cramped environs. It highlights, too, man's ability to alter to his taste the natural environment and create in the process a beautiful contemplative corner of the universe. Nature and art, like gardens and cities, are, as they have been for the past 20 centuries, easily intertwined.

And, for better or for worse, the regal bronze sculpture will remain long after the sedges and rushes have gone to seed.

The long north view showing the narrow garden, as it existed. The sculpture is tucked in between two house wings, far right.

In a sunny position across from the kitchen wing, table and chairs occupy the original site intended for the sculpture. Instead, the art piece was moved nearer the house, for enjoyment of a close view.

The bronze nymph, sculpted by Aristides Demetrios, rests serenely between two wings of the house.

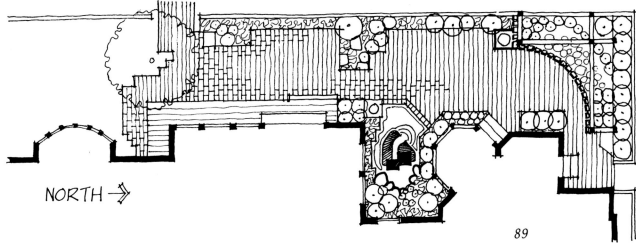

NORTH →

An
Old Dowager
by Sutro Forest

In the 1930s, Rosita Levy summarized her garden objectives and accomplishments for the San Francisco Garden Club. Her speech tells only half the story. Today, her once-magnificent garden broods over its forested site, awaiting restoration and more than a footnote in the annals of San Francisco gardens and gardening.

Spring arrives on cue each February when plum trees awaken in the forest as Mrs. Levy intended. Her flair for the dramatic is evident here, as in the eerie reminders of her garden costume parties which linger two decades after her departure. This garden, to the neighborhood children and generations removed, will always be the Rosita Levy garden.

On the quiet city street outside her garden, an avenue of plum trees lines the brick-paved cul-de-sac. These street refinements are credited in part to Rosita Levy; her gardening interest spilled over her garden boundary line and continues to give pleasure to street strollers every spring.

To hear Rosita Levy tell the story of her garden-making in 1908 on this site is to understand why the slope of this mountain challenges gardeners years later. "The land was covered with poison oak, sage and blackberry vines; the soil, solid red rock . . . the ground is sloping and there were very few places where you could get a secure foothold." Her intricate stone terraces tamed the hillside; beneath the existing pines she planted ferns, cineraria, columbine, rhododendron, hydrangeas and clematis.

She took advantage of the steep slope by introducing a waterfall which cascaded to a pond surrounded by woodwardia, moss, "a profusion" of forget-me-nots, and a pussy willow tree fashioned from an offshoot rooted in water.

The terraces remain (only recently uncovered), the waterworks no longer cascade, while the plants and pines have all but disappeared under the canopy of the advancing eucalyptus forest, planted by pioneer Adolph Sutro before the turn of the century.

Without the tightly-knit neighborhood association of which she was so much a part, this garden and its history might have been lost to succeeding generations. An old photograph album recently surfaced, held for years by the daughter of an old friend, now links the current owners, newly arrived from Chicago, with the past, after a two-year search for a history of their site.

It gives one pause to think of the treasure chests hidden away in San Francisco basements and attics; these secret chronicles of garden fashions and moods, just waiting for daylight.

Viewed from the tiled terrace, the trees and shrubs cast shadow where once the sun came through.

The teahouse, too, survives from Rosita Levy's garden, even though her estate has been carved into smaller lots.

Surviving the old garden, an old Oriental bridge leads nowhere, but reminds the new owners of garden parties in days gone by.

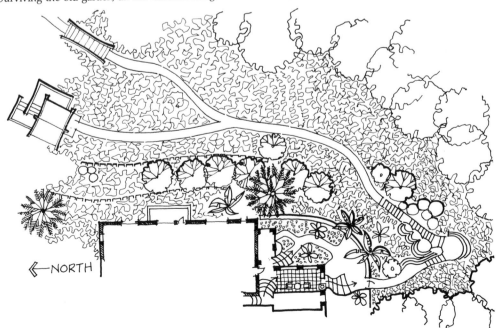

←NORTH

*A
Thomas Church
Design
On Russian Hill*

The shortest distance between two points—in this case, two long, low city decks—is, naturally, a straight line. But for this north-facing garden on the crest of Russian Hill, a carefully conceived *curved* pathway, off center, was the simple, restrained design solution created by landscape architect Thomas Church twenty years ago.

Mr. Church, the nationally-acclaimed garden designer, lived and gardened around the corner from this Russian Hill site. He accepted this challenge late in his career precisely because this city neighborhood was so near and dear, and also because his long-time colleague, architect William Wurster, sought his advice. The masterful result is wholly intact two decades later, in part because the original owner still treasures the rich rewards of that two-hour consultation with one of the country's leading garden designers.

To stroll through this oblong garden takes but 20 leisurely paces. With the sound of crushed gravel underfoot, one wanders past a crisp, white candytuft edging that defines the beds of gracious camellias, regal rhododendrons and two hundred spring bulbs. The tiny hilltop house is skillfully enlarged by its long low deck, which leads, in turn to the graceful curved pathway. The garden gradually flows to the lower 'sun trap' deck at the far end of the garden. No space here for tiny little secret garden rooms, just one straightforward outdoor room designed by a confident and competent landscape architect.

How did the curved walkway materialize? "He took a hose and curved it around for the path; that's how he did it! He just put the hose down once, very simple," recounts owner Tova Wiley. And how did Mr. Church design the low glass-enclosed platform that traps the sun at the lower end of the yard? "On the back of an envelope." The rounded pathway gives the garden width and perspective and lulls the visitor into thinking the garden is larger than it actually is—a fine design principle handed down from Mr. Church to Mrs. Wiley and others with small narrow plots of land. Until the plan was in place, the owner had agonized over the shady, sloping "jungle" just outside her living room windows. "When you have a good plan and the beds are laid out and self-contained, you can then decide what to do in a little area," Mrs. Wiley observes. "A talented landscape designer has learned to use space to an advantage. It's just like a house . . . if you have a good plan in your house and use the space properly, why you have a successful structure. If people tried to design their own houses they'd get a mish-mash, a mess. I think the same is true of the garden."

The initial outlay is more than justified, in Mrs. Wiley's opinion, in the years of satisfaction which follow. "You divide the cost by the number of years you enjoy the garden and it just comes to nothing; it's like buying a good suit of clothes—pay a good price for it, wear it a long time, then divide by the number of years you wear it. You'll find it costs very little!"

The plantings are Mrs. Wiley's. Hers is admittedly a spring garden, not unlike an East Coast garden with its deciduous trees and elaborate spring bulb display. The blossoms arrive almost two months earlier in San Francisco than in many Northern spring gardens, and freezing temperatures are not the constant threat here by the sea than in many parts of the country. Without frosts and chill, however, many traditional bulbs—tulips particularly—will not come back year after year as many garden catalogues promise. This is the first setback for so many San Francisco gardeners, so Mrs. Wiley plants her spent spring bulbs (after chilling them in the fridge for at least two months prior to planting) the following fall in the cooler outlying countryside.

Barring a friend or house in the country, the only solution for many San Franciscans is to substitute South African, Mediterranean or Australasian bulbs which thrive in similar seaside conditions. Easier said than done? Not for Mrs. Wiley, who advises newcomers to seek out, as she did years ago, the Strybing Arboretum garden lectures, held in Golden Gate Park throughout the year. For years, Mrs. Wiley managed the annual Strybing Arboretum plant sale and is considered one of the city's expert plantswomen. She offers these two insights into gardening in small city spaces: as long as the garden is swept clean and appears neat and tidy, it won't matter how many lush plants are spread throughout the garden; and frequent doses of ground-up kitchen scraps provide most of the nourishment needed for plants (potted particularly) in this confined area. At one of those garden lectures 20 years ago, Mrs. Wiley heard Emily Brown, the author of *Landscaping With Perennials,* mention that the perennial evergreen candytuft (*Iberis sempervirens*) makes a superb, neat, low edging plant in this city. The two flats of candytuft purchased after the lecture have survived decades of shearings and storms and wind and change in the beds beyond. In spring bloom, the edging is 'like a white ruffle.'

The beds beyond are filled with bulbs ordered from the best catalogues; while the bulbs and catalogues may change from year to year, the planting routine remains the same: Thanksgiving Day is spring bulb planting day! Ruthlessly replacing the blooming impatiens, the spring bulbs go into their allotted niches in the mid and lower beds—the upper bed against the house is too shady for bulbs.

With no space to hide away the imperfections and open trenchwork of a dedicated gardener, small gardens must pay the price of the changing seasons, with the handsome payoff a season or two away. A little soil showing is the reminder to this gardener that spring is yet to come, that in this city which, some say, is without seasons, all four seasons are in fact well represented, thanks to informed planning and planting.

Spring, however, is the celebrated season here. And the design is visually intact, as Mr. Church envisioned in one of his last private San Francisco garden commissions, on the hill he so loved. As many

The sun trap terrace, at the far end of the garden, opens to the eastern view of Coit Tower on Telegraph Hill.

The 'Akebono' cherry tree reaches its peak the last week in March, when bulbs enhance the spring scene.

The curved walkway, with its candy tuft border, as Thomas Church laid it out 25 years ago with garden hose in hand. This view is from the sun trap terrace looking south toward the house.

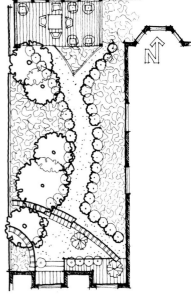

of his city gardens succumb to successive ownerships—with a minor modification here, a total transformation there—this Russian Hill garden is a clear reminder of Tommy Church's cool, creative vision for small gardens everywhere.

_A
Romantic
Scented Hillside
Overlooking
Downtown_

Were it not for the skyscrapers looming on the immediate horizon, this romantic country garden could be set miles, even oceans, away. On the east slope of Russian Hill, this enormous garden spills down the hillside, creating many moods and sending out wonderful fragrances as it winds its way down the steep slope. The seasonal scents invoke memories of more carefree times and remind this city gardener, who is a children's author and storyteller, of centuries of myth and tradition surrounding perfume and plants in the garden.

'Harmony Hill' is a short 10-minute walk from the financial district, yet the garden seems frozen in time, steeped in history. The aura is created less from old existing plantings—'Harmony Hill' is one of the oldest gardens on the hill—but from new plantings designed to invoke days gone by.

The steepness of the site was the greatest barrier to rejuvenation five years ago when 'Harmony Hill' needed a fresh start. The ascent from the street below takes dozens of steps just to reach the front garden gate, and many more steps lead to the front door and hillside behind the gabled shingle home. The back slope was hardly visible under mounds of ivy and blackberry. The tangle smothered everything in its path, and its green presence helped delay the inevitable overhaul.

The transformation came after a one hour consultation—on site—with a nurseryman from nearby Magic Gardens; the professional advice proved to be the turning point for this gardener. The slope, she learned, needed terracing in order to hold the roots of finer plants; that done, she could turn attention to scented plants and their placement up-slope (and downwind) from the sunny back garden where luncheon and tea are frequently served. She knew that a "boring" garden filled with flats of seasonal "instant" color was not for her; the professional advice gave her new avenues to explore.

Unusual fragrant varieties of dependable San Francisco shrubs—camellias and rhododendrons for example—now take their place alongside the tea table. Here, a hedge of _Camellia Sasanqua 'Snow Flake'_ shelters a row of semi-dwarf Rhododendron _'Dora Amateis';_ both filter their fragrance at tea time, the camellia in winter, when interest is so needed. Drifts from _Daphne odora_ and from the spicy wintersweet shrub, _Chimonanthus praecox,_ permeate the hillside in winter.

Scented vines save space while clothing and camouflaging intrusive concrete and wooden walls. A noble, twining, wisteria drapes its perfumed blossoms over the back door in spring; this relatively young but long-lived plant will continue to announce high spring for generations to come. The heavy perfume of the lacy pink jasmine, _Jasminum polyanthum,_ drifts from the arbor near the foot of the stairs, and shares spring bloom with a rambunctious white potato vine, _Solanum jasminoides,_ which, despite its name, has no scent.

One of the owner's favorite and most subtle scents comes from the beguiling, mounding plants of heliotrope, the old fashioned flower from Peru. The quiet color blends well with other blues in the garden, and a mound of this charming flower greets visitors, at eye level, by the front gate, announcing the special interest beyond. Only one flower, however, is needed to announce the gardenia-like presence of the rare _Luculia gratissima_ shrub near the front door, halfway up the slope at the center landing.

As the blue wisteria and pink jasmine fade, and scented rhododendrons fill the air, white star jasmine (_Trachelospermum jasminoides_) takes over in summer. In fall, drifts of tiny autumn-blooming crocus poke through the soil beneath the apple tree growing against the protected southeast wall of the house. As each scent fades, the memories dim, only to be reawakened at the next season with new perfumes. The rejuvenation is constant, from framework to fragrances; all this, the result of a one-hour house call, and continuing consultation with tree surgeon Ted Kipping, landscape designer Stephen Suzman and landscape plantsman Jon Barlow.

Satisfied that each season has its share of successes, the owner, an author of children's books, will now turn her attention to the stories and myths behind the plants and their scents. To show the children, first hand, the garden classics is the completion of the cycle of rejuvenation, the reawakening of senses in the city, where senses are so often dulled by inhuman scale.

Viewed from downtown skyscrapers facing north, this Russian Hill garden comes into plain view, with its enormous green cover and lush surrounds—an island of green in a built-up city. Viewed even closer, from the garden gate, this scented garden unveils sophisticated possibilities on a small city slope.

An old scented rhododendron in the front garden, underplanted with Baby Tear.

The forget-me-nots, which carpet the upper slopes in spring, came from one packet of seed scattered years ago by the owner's daughter. Each spring, the flowers reappear.

Wisteria drapes over the upper terrace and perfumes the garden in March.

Beneath graceful tree fern, scented rhododendron and heliotrope spill down the entry garden.

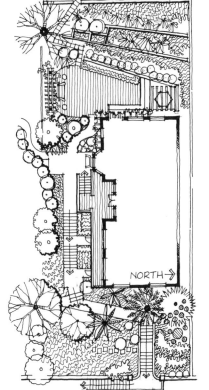

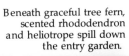

NORTH →

An Old
Rose Garden
in Glen Park

Blowzy old roses, relaxed and rambling, went out of fashion for a while, as do many flower fads. Gardening fads normally skip a generation or two in their leap from prominence to obscurity; add to this our mobility today, and the chances become remote of finding a city garden an entire generation removed. The forgotten and neglected corners likely to harbor old plant species in country and suburban gardens are rare in tight city spaces. Unwanted and unloved plants, are pulled by each succeeding city owner, leaving little hope for wallflowers to wait on the sidelines until fashions change once again.

In this Glen Park garden, then, the miracle is that not only did the old roses survive successive owners and years, but that, 7 years ago, newlyweds Ann Hiaring and Morgan Hall had the vision to temporarily, then permanently, preserve the precious old plants in their midst. With no previous knowledge or interest in old (or even new) roses, this thoroughly modern couple has now built up perhaps the most enviable collection of antique and old-fashioned roses in the city.

Glen Park—named after the spectacular steep ravine and park nearby—was a sleepy cow pasture four miles southwest of downtown when the 1906 earthquake struck. Streams of refugees took up residence in wooden cottages which lined the narrow streets. Protected by the wind barriers of Diamond Heights and Twin Peaks, the neighborhood soon flourished with turn-of-the-century roses covering arbors and picket fences.

It is these roses—the shell-pink, early hybrid tea, 'Madame Caroline Testout'; the flame offspring of 'Mamon Cochet', 'Niles Cochet'; and the endearing 'Cecile Brunner' found in warm climates around the globe—that give the neighborhood distinction. Some of these very same roses in the path of bulldozers would have been lost but for preservation by these newlyweds. Both of the 'Madame Caroline Testout' roses here, for example, were rescued from vacant lots and extinction nearby. Plucky Madame Testout, the 19th Century dress designer who boldly approached a French rose breeder to name a rose in her honor, would like to know that this rose, unavailable in nearby nurseries, is safe for another generation.

Presiding over the rare rose collection is the faded, pale pink beauty, the rose that remained to inspire once again, the turn-of-the-century hybrid gigantea, 'Belle of Portugal'. A San Francisco favorite for years because of its early (and remarkably long) bloom and its preference for warm winters, this floppy rose fell out of favor when upright, formal, repeat-flowering hybrid tea roses became the rage. The challenge for the new owners was discovering just which rose they had inherited, and what its requirements might be. The identity of another San Francisco favorite, the exquisite, scented pink rose 'Cecile Brunner' rambling by the kitchen door was easier to come by, as local nurseries still carry this 'Sweetheart' rose.

The garden's fate was sealed when a friend introduced Ann Hiaring to the writings of Gertrude Jekyll, the Englishwoman whose passion for subtle rose color and informal gardening style inspired so many of her countrymen around the turn of the century.

The front entry garden went in first ("You'll feel better, your neighbors will too" a friend advised), and then, after their small cottage was remodeled, it was time to tackle the cement pathways and shallow soil in the sheltered back yard which was once a chicken yard. Rather than jackhammer all the hard pathways, Mr. Hall, an architect and contractor, built wooden walkways and brick landings above the harsh cement surfaces, thereby adding different garden levels for interest. All the while working around the magnificent 'Belle of Portugal' rose, he then added two small lawns, trellises and raised beds to hide an unattractive retaining wall. With the backbone in place, the garden was now ready for the 50 roses yet to come.

The old rose collection soon spilled on to the adjacent lot, the shrubs and ramblers allowed to wander at will. Rose gardens needn't be stiff and formal, Ann Hiaring says; roses should be used as garden furnishings, as flowering shrubs, as all-year beauty. The flowers themselves are ruffled and many-petalled, reminders of a bygone era, when her favorite roses 'Charles de Mills' and 'Madame Alfred Carriere' enjoyed their heyday. The colors, too, are subtle, not splashy, and keep their vibrancy in the overcast by the sea. The fragrant hybrid Musk, 'Buff Beauty', for example, remains a handsome apricot in the San Francisco fog while elsewhere it fades in the noonday sun. While colors remain true, the many-petalled flowers often succumb to mildew in this damp maritime climate—single, 5-petalled roses are best grown near the sea, the San Francisco experts advise. The Hiaring-Hall garden of many-petalled roses would, at first glance, disprove the mildew theory were it not that this garden is protected from the fog which permeates neighborhoods only a half mile to the west.

Not all the roses in this garden are old or out of date. Modern introductions—particularly the Wilhelm Kordes (and sons) introductions from Germany—are allowed, because breeding has produced roses that appear old fashioned, but in fact are excellent repeat performers, or heavily scented, or otherwise well-behaved. The delicate, single Kordes rose 'Sparrieshoop', introduced in 1953, is a favorite here, along with Mr. Kordes fluffy 'Lavender Lassie', a 1960 hybrid Musk.

Even new rose introductions go out of fashion and fade from view, once nurseries and breeders give up carrying a particular rose. The 1972 hybrid tea aptly named 'Golden Gate', for example, is already out of fashion, no longer available even from its breeder, Jackson and Perkins of Oregon. But the clear yellow 'Golden Gate' rose, saved from a friend's cast-offs, thrives in a sheltered position below the east-facing porch and now becomes another rose saved in a garden full of "savelings", as Anne Hiaring calls her roses.

The translucent pink 'Belle of Portugal' rose, right, a remnant from previous owners, dominates the back garden during the beginning of the rose season each April.

The archway, which leads to the vacant field once filled with Ann Hiaring's 'saveling' roses, is smothered in 'Felicite et Perpetue' and 'Rambling Rector' roses later in the season.

The front entry, with roses and rosemary, wisteria and scented 'savelings'.

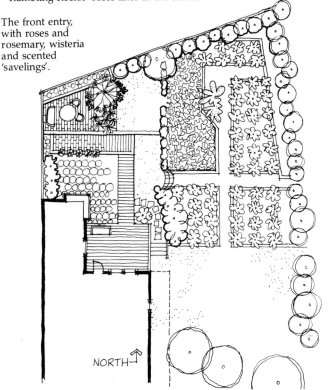

NORTH

Many of her roses, however, are rare turn-of-the-century introductions or earlier, bloom early and mid-season, and might not repeat but hold their blossoms well. After years of collecting, Ann Hiaring insists that catalogue shopping is essential ("the local nurseries just carry junk"), and that membership in Heritage Roses, a national organization with local affiliates, is equally important for the exchange of plants and ideas.

The mood in this garden, and in the neighborhood remains country, and the surrounds are now enhanced by the preservation efforts of the newest Glen Park residents. One small part of a city's heritage, is, for the time being, vibrantly alive. Madame Caroline Testout, who never lived to see the city of Portland, Oregon, line the sidewalks with her rose, would approve of the San Francisco preservation effort. She might not even mind sharing the rose spotlight, in this case, with 59 other rose introductions.

*A California
Native Plant
Garden
on Mt. Davidson*

Long before gold was discovered in the foothills beyond San Francisco Bay, the golden flowers that covered the hills in spring had already been discovered by British, French and Russian explorers. While ships came to call on Presidio commanders, eager botanists bolted for the hills and set about naming new-found plants after one another. The golden California poppy thus was christened *Eschscholzia* (pronounced Esh-*sholts*-ee-a) after Dr. Johann Friedrich Eschscholz, the Russian plant hunter. His traveling companion and fellow botanist, Adelbert von Chamisso, is remembered in the *Lupinus chamissonis*—the Dune Lupine found in coastal sands.

Each city has its story to tell of magnificent virgin countryside now paved over and otherwise forgotten; San Francisco's mostly treeless terrain nonetheless held a vast array of flowering plants during the Indian and later, Spanish and Mexican, periods which preceded the gold strike of 1849. This Mt. Davidson garden is not only a refuge for San Francisco's native plants (and a tribute to the plant hunters who discovered and distributed the extraordinary coastal collection), but a compact historical view of the entire early California landscape.

The humble origin for this ambitious restoration came only a decade ago after San Francisco tree surgeon Ted Kipping realized that native flowers and grasses near his boyhood home on Mt. Davidson— the tallest San Francisco "hill" at 938 ft.—were disappearing rapidly in the wake of the bulldozers. In addition, his parents often visited the natural canyons and meadows on Mt. Tamalpais, the higher peak just north of the Golden Gate Bridge. Thus, the idea of recreating, for his parents, the plants of "Mt. Tam" alongside the plants of the San Francisco sand dunes and hills took hold. Soon thereafter, annual flowers rarely found in this city's cultivated gardens, but well loved and nurtured in gardens abroad, filled the hillside with vivid displays while the native trees and shrubs grew to maturity.

The flowering year begins in early February with the emergence of the tiny cream-colored Star Lily, *Zigadenus fremontii,* from bulbs. The flowering currents, *Ribes* spp., also begin the new year in blossom.

In March and April, spring—California's showiest, but by no means its only, wildflower season,— arrives with the yellows of annual buttercups (*Ranunculus* spp.) and Meadow Foam, known in Britain as Poached Egg Flower (*Limnanthes douglasii*). The native blues are here in iris bulbs (*Iris douglasiana*— another plant named after the Scottish explorer, David Douglas), in California Blue-eyed Grass (*Sisyrinchium* spp.) and the California wild lilac shrubs, *Ceanothus* spp. Less well-known and rarely cultivated in coastal gardens, the native Miner's Lettuce (*Montia perfoliata*) is a particular favorite of the owner, for its tiny green collar surrounding clusters of pink and white flowers, and its ability to slowly fill in spaces occupied by the iris and, later, the summer broadiaeas.

The open, sloping meadow outside the kitchen window is filled with native bunchgrasses which are harvested just before prime, then dried for year-round arrangements. The meadow gradually climbs the hill and meets the sheltered, shaded plateau at the site of a handsome 35-ft. willow tree. The grey-trunked willow has grown in 20 years from a single slip in a bouquet presented as a gift to the owner. Unlike shrubby suckering willow relatives, this slip, rooted in water, has been carefully pruned over the years to a single leader trunk with sturdy secondary branches arching over the two distinct habitats at its base. Willows are wonderful soil stabilizers along muddy banks, and this hillside willow anchors the upper 'forest' to the lower 'meadow.'

The son refrained from planting a host of other California trees on the small site—city dwellers so often ignore ultimate dimensions—but couldn't resist adding one native conifer, the California Nutmeg, *Torreya californica.* Opposite the nutmeg tree, a Quaking Aspen (*Populus tremuloides*), native to the Sierras and other western mountains, shimmers and rustles in the breezes before turning color and dropping its leaves in autumn. What began as two seaside habitats soon spread to encompass plants from the distant Sierras across the vast state of California.

Under the protection of the trees and a thick, yearly top-dressing, the Yerba Buena herb—named after the "good herb" which covered the village of Yerba Buena before it was renamed San Francisco in 1847—makes a fragrant carpet on the upper knoll. The spongey top-dressing comes right off the tree surgeon's truck at the end of the working day; annually, more than 6 in. is added to the hardpan clay soil in order to produce 1 in. of dark brown, rich soil.

The subtle scent and blue flowers of California wild lilacs (*Ceanothus*), grown and appreciated in temperate climates and warm positions worldwide, are represented in this garden by several shrubs: *C. Hearstiorum* (saved from the Hearst Castle farther down the coast), *C. thyrsiflorus,* the coastal Blue Blossom, and *C. griseus,* the Carmel Creeper.

In summer, the mood changes as the fog rolls in to blanket the meadow and knoll. The tall yellow spires of native Evening Primrose (*Oenethera hookerii*) occupy the base of the willow tree where Meadow Foam once stood. Translucent pink cup-shaped flowers of Farewell-to-Spring (*Clarkia amonea*) spill down the meadow and announce that summer has arrived in the countryside and in the city as well. A newly-installed timed mist system encourages profuse summer flowering, helping to recreate the moister California environments where late summer wildflowers flourish.

Native Plant Societies have multiplied in California and elsewhere during the past 25 years in an effort to preserve remnants of America's original landscape. In just one city garden, San Francisco's flowering sand dunes, coastal bluffs, laurel and oak groves are brought back to life, not only in spring, but in the winter rain, summer fog and bright autumn sunshine. "All over this state there are things that

View from the kitchen window transports the kitchen-bound into the country, with its hillsides in April bloom.

Yellows and blues carpet the sunny Kipping hillside in April. Above, under the shade of the willow tree, shade lovers thrive.

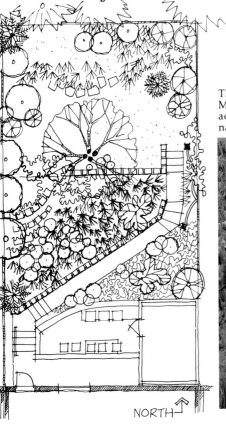

The city view hardly hints at the country mood of this Mt. Davidson garden. A thick top-dressing of compost is added to the soil yearly. A rare Quaking Aspen tree, native to the Sierras, thrives alongside ribes and iris.

Delphinium variegatum, in spring bloom.

In summer, 'Farewell to Spring' (*Clarkia amoena*) signals the change of season in the Kipping Garden.

NORTH

99

bloom in the summer and that bloom in the fall. The trick is to bring them all together in one garden," Ted Kipping notes. Bringing nearby and distant environments into one small, sloping, compact city garden is an easy trick, which, in the end, not only permits the owner to savour the wilds, but save the wild things simultaneously.

A MAY GARDEN

A Banana Belt Garden Above Mission Dolores

High above Mission Dolores, this old estate on Dolores Heights rests serene in its surroundings, like its plantings so well suited to the warmth of the east side. Long ago, owner Linna Kaye learned that a good gardener plants not those plants suited to the gardener, but rather those plants best suited to the local climate and conditions.

Begonias and heathers, for example, were particular favorites of Mrs. Kaye's 34 years ago when she moved from the San Francisco fog belt to this sunny hilltop two miles away. The weather is remarkably warmer and drier at the inland site, the soil not as sandy or fast-draining—the begonias were in strange surroundings.

A new start was needed, but how to learn which plants to try? The first necessary ingredient was courage to admit that after years of gardening, this gardener was stumped. Next, classes at a nearby university revealed local do's and don'ts and also introduced her to lifelong horticultural friends, including her gardener of 30 years, Gus Broucaret.

The best San Francisco plants—camellias, roses, hydrangeas—are clipped into hedges set against the old wooden house and verandah. The sunny east-facing house is shaded by magnificent tall rhododendrons, climbing wisteria and 'Cecile Brunner' roses. The protected entry court is a showcase for tender temperamental specimens of Daphne, the envy of every San Francisco gardener. Mrs. Kaye shrugs at her success with the daphnes, and reveals another gardening secret: try all four exposures (north, south, east, west) for new, special, plants. One siting, she maintains, is bound to be superior, particularly in small city gardens where shadow and sunlight create vest-pocket environments.

Daphnes are short lived in Mrs. Kaye's garden. Every few years, new cuttings come from branches of the parent plant to assure a constant supply; extra cuttings are shared with friends. Replacing other favorite plants isn't quite as easy because, she says, nurserymen no longer carry old standbys, plants popular three decades ago.

While Mrs. Kaye needed help with specific plants, she knew which style she wanted: relaxed and informal. Viewed from the east-facing verandah, the weeping, scented, locusts (*Robinia pseudoacacia*) combine with lacy maples, purple plums and hawthorn trees to shade the wide lawn in the morning. Up against the verandah, a hedge of *Camellia japonica* is kept clipped to the height of the railing, allowing porch-sitters to enjoy the expanse of lawn and garden. Climbing the east face of the house, a magnificent 'Cecile Brunner' rose reaches for the second story and sends out scented pink blossoms every April and May. By then, the nearby wisteria vine is past its prime but the loose foliage continues to soften the house lines.

On the south edge of the long winding lawn, a white picket fence separates the food garden from the ornamental garden. In this sun-drenched plot, Mrs. Kaye grows exotic and everyday vegetables and fruits remembered from her childhood in the tropics and from her husband's family farm on the Peninsula. Kiwi vines mingle with Eureka lemons ("I like the flavor better than the Meyer lemon"), which stand near the tree tomatoes (*Cyphomandra betacea*), a specialty of this garden.

Between the lawn and the house, a fine hedge of hydrangea blooms in June, bringing to an end the spring season. Every 4 years, the hydrangea hedge is pruned way back ("I hate to do it," Mrs. Kaye admits) to keep the fluffy flower heads at eye level. Pruning, in this garden, is always subtle, never severe, so that few clues exist of the necessary shrub and tree shaping. The constant attention to pruning details eliminates the need for one drastic cut-back. The peak hydrangea bloom, like an hourglass or sundial, reminds Mrs. Kaye to send anniversary congratulations to relatives married beside her hydrangea blossoms years ago.

Although 34 spring seasons have come and gone on Dolores Heights for this octogenarian, Mrs. Kaye continues to learn and experiment in the four different exposures, with her dozens of trees, shrubs, scented flowers and exotic fruits. She freely shares her enthusiasm and knowledge—an essential ingredient to the continuation of inner city gardening, and to the continuation of neighborhood tradition.

New city gardeners should live with an existing garden, at least through one spring and summer, before tearing out the old and planting the new, Mrs. Kaye advises. Spring is, after all, a time of renewal, a time for hidden bulbs and deciduous leaves to reveal their presence, a time to take stock of one's surroundings. The surrounds in this garden, and in so many other San Francisco gardens, are beautiful and pleasing and harbingers of seasons to come.

The 'Sweetheart' rose, delicately scented and present in many old San Francisco gardens, frames this east view toward Potrero Hill.

The courtyard garden, separated from the main garden by glass doors. Here, in the protection of warm walls, daphne thrives alongside other tender plants.

Roses smother the verandah in spring.

White potted flowers climb the stairs to the front porch, and help define the precipitous stairway edge. Rhododendrons, tall and mature, brighten the already-sunny garden in early May.

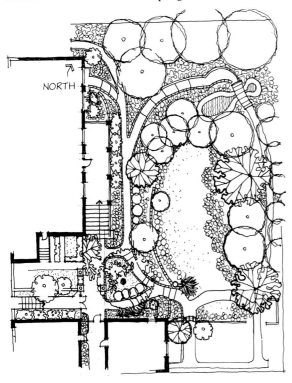

NORTH

A
Rose Garden
in Eureka Valley

When the British, after the Dutch lead, settled South Africa in the 19th century, they brought along their beloved roses and the English passion for gardening. In the process, the parched South African landscape turned leafy and green, while the exotic native flora began to attract worldwide attention. San Francisco, too, began as a treeless landscape, which would, like South Africa's, soon be transformed by waves of immigrants descending upon our sandy shores.

Within the past decade, one South African immigrant, Stephen Suzman, has brought to San Francisco his keen and seemingly effortless sense of gardening; his tiny Eureka Valley garden embodies all that is English and romantic in the mind's eye. Not an inch of earth is spared in his quest to have flowers and shrubs everywhere. The highlight of his flowering year comes in early May when the roses reach their prime.

The east-facing garden, accessible only via a steep, wooden stairway, is divided into two areas, each with its different mood and habitat. The border and bed farthest from the house—and therefore the sunniest spot for bright flowers—is filled with roses, clematis and honeysuckle reaching to smother their nearest companions, each sending up cheery flowers to be viewed from the upstairs windows. The lawn in the center rests the eye and leads it toward the tall pergola, at the far end of the garden, which carries the spring flowers. Rhododendrons, azaleas and ferns cut a path between the lawn and shade garden against the house.

Three climbing roses—'Royal Sunset', 'Sparrieshoop' and 'Lady Forteviot'—arch over the pergola which provides the focus for the surrounding confection. Scattered on the sidelines are roses, mostly 20th Century introductions, grown for dazzle, decoration or novelty.

'Peace', the splashy yellow award-winner from the 1940s, is grown for its superb individual cut flower, even though the bush is not to his liking. 'Chicago Peace', the deeper-toned ("like a sun-burnt Swede, don't you think?"), equally large-flowered sport of the former, is hidden in the north bed so its foliage will recede when it grows leggy. The crinkled rugosa rose, which colonizes East Coast gardens and unfolds its fragrant flowers all summer long, is represented in Mr. Suzman's garden by the muted yellow hybrid 'Agnes' which Mr. Suzman found flowering at the Huntington Botanical Garden in Southern California.

Few of his roses repeat their bloom later in the year, as do so many roses sold today. While rose hybridizers have rushed to breed repeat-flowering roses, and rose enthusiasts have snatched up each new offering, Mr. Suzman instead looks for perfection only once a year. "After all, we don't expect rhododendrons and lilacs to bloom all year round, why roses?" The pioneering spirit, the tendency to be one step ahead of his contemporaries, spills over even into his rose garden.

His previous observations and experience gardening in two countries—South Africa and England—helped establish the style and pace of planting in his San Francisco garden seven years ago. In his sheltered site here, the African Corn Lily (*Ixia*), and the pink Pompon Tree (*Dais continifolia*) remind Mr. Suzman of his homeland. A Snowball (*Viburnum opulus* 'Roseum') went in, too, because it resembled one in his South African garden. The laburnum planted behind the rose arbor brings back memories of his university days at Oxford. "North Oxford is full of laburnum and lilac trees, neither of which grow in South Africa." So San Francisco has taken its turn and in turn this garden has became overcrowded with nostalgic plants, but the experiments are exhilarating for this wise and witty plantsman.

For the few patches of open earth, Mr. Suzman wedges in white tobacco plant (*Nicotiana*), a favorite annual he prefers to the "boring" selection of common annuals (impatiens particularly) offered by many local nurseries. He scolds the breeders, however, for eliminating the fragrance in the dwarf nicotianas now on the market. He observes that in San Francisco's mild climate, annuals often behave like weak perennials, confounding plantsmen.

He readily acknowledges he "overplanted" his garden, but his confessions are meant to stimulate an energetic gardening dialogue rather than to browbeat the gardener at hand. In this remarkable talent, he gives away his heritage. Following the admitted foible, an outrageous statement is then bound to follow—again, as provocation: "I wish the hybridizers would get to work on the dandelions so we could grow them as ornamental plants!" and another: "I find the onion and the oxalis (two of San Francisco worst pests) very pretty weeds—I have a tendency not to pull out plants when they seed themselves because I know they're happy." The invasive bindweed (*Convolvulus arvensis*) is an exception.

Cross breeding furthers science, rose selection, cities in general and city gardens in particular. For every romantic British rose garden, a perfectly proportioned Japanese garden exists in a nearby San Francisco neighborhood. Owners willing to share their heritage and gardening enthusiasm contribute to this diverse and civilized cultural exchange unmatched in outlying, less populated, less compact towns. Mr. Suzman's garden writings and teachings have already won him a devoted following in this city; San Francisco has, then, already reaped the benefit of this cultural exchange.

Beneath the pergola at the far end of the garden, the small lawn and house come into view, framed by climbing roses and nostalgic plantings.

The 'Sweetheart' rose arches, without support, over the stairway leading from the lawn to the shade garden against the house in Eureka Valley.

Climbing roses, mixed with ease, smother the lattice support. 'Royal Sunset', 'Sparrieshoop' and 'Lade Forteviat' make this May show.

103

A Grand Design in Pacific Heights

When a daughter inherits her mother's enormous city garden—and inherits, too, the daily reminders of tennis on the upper lawn in the '20s, or scented roses outside the conservatory door—does the garden become a museum or the daughter's own? Should its grand 1930s garden redesign, one of the last by an architect before landscape architecture came into its own, remain intact or should it change with the times?

These were the decisions facing this daughter—now a grandmother—almost four decades ago when she traded her one-acre, suburban home for this Pacific Heights garden and home of her youth. The garden today remains old-fashioned as designed, yet the daughter's imprint is on every border and in every bed.

The timbered, turn-of-the-century mansion, designed by architect William Curlett (he designed Shreve's and other downtown landmarks) as his own city residence, occupies a prominent corner on one of the lushest blocks in Pacific Heights. The view of the Golden Gate Bridge is ever-present, although many hillside gardens (including this one) are hidden or dominated by the mansions with the views. An open, wrought-iron gate beckons sidewalk strollers to peer through and view the terraced garden; another old-fashioned touch purposely preserved in a neighborhood whose owners have walled off their gardens from public view.

The handsome garden design seen through the gate is not the 1904 original—or even its 1919 alteration in the year the owner's family took possession—but, rather, a 1935 remodel by their neighbor and friend Warren Perry. While attending to a routine top floor remodeling for the family, Mr. Perry, Dean of the Architecture School at the University of California at Berkeley, looked out the window and agreed to redesign the garden below.

In the waning days of an era when architects designed furniture, buildings and landscapes with equal ease and taste, Mr. Perry's bold plan blends perfectly behind this ornate mansion. The inspiration for the dramatic and imposing curved stairway design might well have come to him during one of the operas he attended so regularly in the '30s with his friends down the street.

A magnificent Copper Beech (*Fagus sylvatica* 'Atropunicea') planted on the north property line a generation ago dominates the upper terrace and lawn, where today's gardener once practiced her fore and backhand. A fine collection of tightly-packed, potted orchids thrive under the shade and shelter of the beech tree.

On the opposite end of the old tennis court, across the upper lawn, enormous specimens of her mother's rhododendrons stand beside the English Holly she brought to the city as a slip from her Hillsborough garden. Along the sidelines of the old tennis court, rose standards, underplanted with pink flowers of silver-leaved dianthus, make a neat row to the east.

The seasonal flower border brightens the west. Her mother's preferred red tones have gradually given way to paler, softer colors more to the daughter's liking. At first, however, changes came slowly. "I was scared," she admits.

The flowers of her youth—delphiniums, snapdragons and stock—no longer perform well in this upper bed where a pittosporum hedge now casts its afternoon shadow over her mother's once-sunny lawn. And therein lies the tale of two generations of San Francisco gardeners—the open, treeless landscape of San Francisco's youth is now filled with tall trees and buildings that challenge tree surgeons, neighborhood preservationists and gardeners alike.

On the east-facing slope spilling toward the conservatory and mansion is the curved, divided brick stairway designed by Mr. Perry to replace a straight staircase that limply led from the lower to upper lawn. Two fine specimens of Irish Yew (*Taxus baccata* 'Fastigiata') guard the upper landing and frame the west lawn view from the house. The curvature of the stairway is accentuated with low, horizontal hedges of dwarf cotoneaster, juniper and rosemary, kept constantly clipped to stay within bounds.

At the foot of the stairway is a rounded brick terrace seen by passers-by from the side garden gate. Only a hint of the sweeping summer hydrangea hedge is visible from the street; that massed pink display, created by the daughter from one or two of her mother's original plants, is reserved for invited visitors. Summer by the sea arrives here in June when hydrangeas burst into bloom, making this summer garden, after four decades of trial and error, one of the best in the city.

Seen from the street, the garden gate only hints at the beauty beyond.

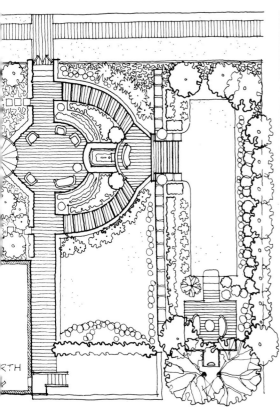

Inside the gate, the design unfolds, with hydrangeas climbing the hillside, left. Irish Yew sentinels separate the lower garden from the upper lawn.

Hydrangeas line the curved stairway, which leads to the upper lawn, where tennis was played long ago.

The site of the tennis court in the 1920s, the owner now tends her summer flower border beside the lawn where once she practiced her tennis game.

*An L-shaped
Garden Room
Near
Lafayette Park*

The many and varied outdoor 'rooms' at Sissinghurst Castle, created in the 1930s by Vita Sackville West and Harold Nicholson in the Kent countryside, served as inspiration for this world traveler when he returned to plan his own city garden. Soon enough this San Franciscan realized that his tiny 33 ft. wide space must be as carefully planned as any of the gardens at Sissinghurst. One city 'room' cannot hide behind hedges when out of bloom, cannot mask the mistakes of early experiments gone awry.

Eight years later, Mr. Paul Wiseman has confirmed the Nicholson assertion that a garden can mature and take its permanent shape after only seven years. He has also proved that copying a concept—in this case, an informal border set against a formal framework—can be as successful as carbon copying another garden, plant for plant.

The formal hedges in both gardens were borne of different necessities. At Sissinghurst, walls needed softening, spaces needed definition. In San Francisco, neighboring laundry, strung much too high and visible from many of the 17 surrounding windows overlooking Mr. Wiseman's plot, immediately jolted the eye so required blotting out. One of the best and most reliable San Francisco hedging plants, Australian Brush Cherry (*Eugenia myrtifolia* or *Syzygium paniculatum*), was immediately called into action to hide the eyesore. Ten specimens were lined up against the north fence, seven against the east fence. The shiny new copper leaves are allowed to thrive above the 4 ft. mark, while their handsome gray trunks are stripped below to create an avenue effect, similar in appearance to the pleached lime walk at Sissinghurst.

The Australian Brush Cherries need a bit of attention in order to keep their neat and compact shape. A quarterly pruning is required for which Mr. Wiseman employs a conventional orchard ladder to keep the tall hedge in good form. An old garden hose, woven through the plants, 8 ft. off the ground, protects the spindly specimens against the wind.

With the backbone in place, Mr. Wiseman set out to recreate the most famous garden room at Sissinghurst: the all-white enclosure, filled with masses of silver, gray and white blossoms and textured leaves. The experiment failed. The white flowers refused to bloom simultaneously; he had wanted the color in late June and July, when the sun reaches highest above neighboring rooftops. He learned two city design lessons in the process: an all white border overwhelmed his miniature space; and spring in San Francisco is better suited to a more subtle splash of white. Only two white plants—tall tulips underplanted with massed candytuft—are needed to create the spring mood.

He has learned, too, to overplant early in the season (mid-March for late June bloom), then thin as needed, rather than to fill in telltale gaps later. The tulips are pulled and discarded after the last bloom fades; Mr. Wiseman advises against watching bulbs brown and wither in small city gardens.

Billowing, carefree borders, with plants spilling over boundaries, are played against tall eugenia sentinels—carried out with utmost care by this interior designer, whose eye for scale and color serves him well. Small details—down to the patio's brick design with volunteer plants creeping through—are also copied from this world famous garden to the south and east of London.

Recreating, plant by plant, a magnificent garden can prove disastrous if the scale and setting is off. This city garden owes its success, first to the Sissinghurst creators, then to the designer who brought home the principles and applied them with intelligence and restraint.

The far corner of the garden receives the first summer sun, where the flower border reaches its peak at the end of June and in July.

In a shaded corner, where sun rarely penetrates, the evergreens frame the flower borders beyond. Note close-cropped eugenia hedge, right, against boundary.

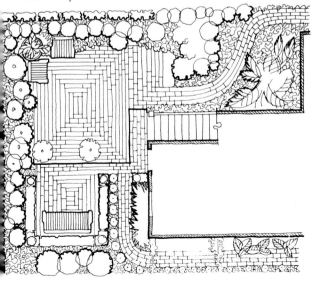

Eugenia (*Syzgium paniculatum*) hedges, clipped close against the open trellis fence underplanted with bright summer flowers.

Every city has its foremost plantsman, one knighted in inside circles as the expert to consult on matters green and growing. Victor Reiter was San Francisco's appointed master and he carried his title with a firm but tender grasp, only occasionally looking up from his breeding journal to realize the whole town was talking about his botanical and horticultural prowess.

Mr. Reiter's sheltered and sloping one-acre garden at the foot of Mt. Sutro is like no other in this city; the size alone, combined with his extraordinary plant collection, made this a "must see" for visiting garden enthusiasts. The octogenarian's passing during production of this book only sharpens the debate over whether his garden—or any garden—is but one man's creation, destined for a new life of decline or redesign, and, further, whether garden preservation should occupy a more prominent role in conservation efforts, as it does abroad.

Fortunately for San Francisco, this spacious garden is now in the hands of Mr. Reiter's widow and children who share his keen interest in the land and its upkeep. For one brief moment, however, on a crisp fall 1986 day soon after Mr. Reiter's passing, the garden was in the hands (and knees) of a most distinguished clean-up crew—one San Francisco Parks chief, one Pacific Horticulture magazine editor, and dozens of others untitled but no less expert—gathered to help family members keep weeds at bay for one more season. It was an astonishing, affectionate outpouring in tribute to Mr. Reiter.

Hundreds of rare plants once thrived here; many survive his years of collecting. Collecting was, for Mr. Reiter, an all-consuming hobby, a chance to bring back a one-of-a-kind specimen, a chance to shelter outdated, unpopular hybrids until fashions changed once again. He had the space, the knowledge, and, finally, the horticultural connections to make collecting a joy. Each plant has a fascinating history behind its place in this garden—smuggled alpine seeds from the bank president's wife, rare cemetery tree slips, and everywhere gifts and exchanges from friends. These stories, in later years, became the focus for garden visitors, became almost as important as the plants themselves.

A turning point for this garden—and gardener—came with an unexpected chill in December 1932. In Mr. Reiter's words: "The Big Freeze drove the dirt gardeners out of their burrows most successfully... the unprecedented icy blasts from out of the Arctic swept over Northern California leaving its gardens ravaged and its gardeners broken hearted." Thus the California Horticultural Society was born out of resolve of Mr. Reiter and other early participants to "pattern some of the features of our fledgling after that great organization—the Royal Horticultural Society—whose objective is the advancement of horticulture in all its branches."

While some gardeners collect the biggest and brightest new plants, Mr. Reiter wanted the smallest, most subtle, oldest breeds. For new plants, he bred his own, on site, then offered them for sale in his LaRochette nursery, which his father started years before. Roses were the specialty in the early LaRochette days before Mr. Reiter Jr. advanced to strictly temperate climate specialties, including that most colorful and tender of San Francisco plants—fuchsias. The 1952 LaRochette catalogue is a fuchsia connoisseur's prize in itself, with its enthusiastic listing of introductions that are now scattered in gardens all over San Francisco and elsewhere. He set a goal to breed a fine white fuchsia which appeared in 1949: Fuchsia 'Flying Cloud'—a double rosy white. He then moved on to challenges among the heucheras, echeverias, correas and brooms. Remnants of LaRochette Nursery appear everywhere in this garden— from the masses of fuchsias haphazardly strewn about the upper garden to the lathhouses and greenhouse foundations near the once-bustling 'office' behind the house.

A magnificent tree—a wedding present from a British well wisher—now dominates the upper garden. When the *Magnolia campbellii mollicomata* is in bloom in mid-February, friends gather to toast its magnificence. In Victor Reiter's opinion, this Himalayan Magnolia tree, with its enormous, clear, deep pink blossoms, was the handsomest in the city. The tree arrived as a three-year-old and had to be rerouted through Canada along the way.

So rarified is the atmosphere in this plant collection beneath Mt. Sutro, one is immediately tempted to inquire about seeing the family 'jewels'—Rhododendron 'Victor Reiter Sr.', Fuchsia 'Mrs. Victor Reiter', Echeveria 'Carla Reiter', Fuchsia 'Carla'—until it becomes clear that this unassuming family would prefer showcasing other families' gems. Besides, having a plant named in one's honor is a mixed blessing: if the plant does poorly, the honoree is blamed, rather than the supplier, or the real culprit, which might be a snail or a slug. For this reason, and others, Mr. Reiter preferred to name his new plants according to color, shape or size—characteristics rather than characters.

Each plant, each family has its colorful history at every turn in the garden. Sadly, Mr. Reiter never wrote all the stories down, never strolled through his vast garden with tape recorder in hand, so some memories are lost forever—a lesson other collectors might note. Mr. Reiter's tremendous photo collection, however, equals the best of family albums and chronicles his life work on 35 mm slides, many on permanent view at Strybing's Horticultural Library.

This private garden could hardly be duplicated today—as with any fine collection, it took years to gather and adapt. To see so many different flowering plants in one unscientific setting is enough to send the uninitiated along the collecting path at once; for the initiated, the paths led to Utopia. Unfortunately, becuse Mr. Reiter collected the tiniest species, they are the first to succumb to the weeds, the first to be smothered under larger less desirable plants nearby.

Nature, ever so quickly, closes in. Cities, just as quickly, lose their living collections.

Looking back toward the house and office, which once housed the LaRochette Nursery. A climbing 'Lady Hillingdon' rose gracefully drapes over a wall; the magnolia tree, a wedding present, right.

Hundreds of tiny plants bloom side by side on the upper slope. Mr. Reiter was as proud of his stone work separating each area as he was of the plant collection itself. (Photo by Victor Reiter, courtesy Strybing Arboretum Society)

The mood changes from one area to the next in the vast Victor Reiter garden. This path leads away from the house toward the open, sunny rock garden beyond.

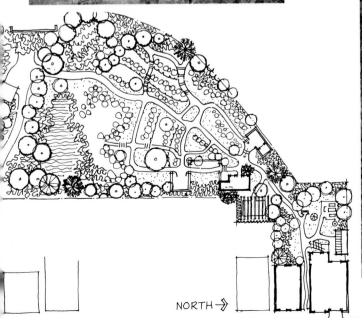

NORTH →

A Garden for the Birds on Telegraph Hill

On a precipitous cliff on a very famous hill, above the city waterfront, invited guests hover over this garden as if it were their own. The refuge is a man-made oasis in a sea of concrete and the visitors know it. They flock here from miles away, as they have for a quarter of a century. This city garden is for the birds.

Created by conservationist Grace deLaet on the crest of Telegraph Hill, the garden shelters at least 24 bird species, some migratory, some year-round residents. Mrs. deLaet uses the most elementary lures to attract them: masses of bright, nectar-rich flowers in curved beds surrounding a shallow, clear stand of water three feet off the ground. The bird bath brings them in, the nectar is their rich reward. Store-bought bird feeders round out the array, although the seed and suet are adjunct rather than essential, in Mrs. deLaet's grand plan.

For more than 20 years, this hilltop gardener has dished out the meals and tended the plants favored by her migrating visitors, and in so doing, has created a distinct San Francisco flyway in the process. The enormous bird population on the southeast face of the hill can be directly traced to this dedicated gardener; she singlehandedly shows that one urban gardener can indeed transform harsh surroundings. Little vegetation existed on the virgin rocky slopes of Telegraph Hill; here, then, is a vast improvement on the 'natural' environment.

Even the basic shrub and tree outline is created with the birds in mind. Tall evergreen trees—of mixed varieties to attract different species—line the west side, while tightly clipped hedging shelters smaller species on the south boundary. Flowering vines smother the north property line to harbor still more refugees.

Four different tree varieties of juniper, eucalyptus, laurel and acacia line her west property line. One tightly-clipped pittosporum hedge provides quick cover along the south boundary line, and flowering vines (honeysuckle, jasmine, trumpet) smother walls and storm-damaged tree trunks. With the exception of a patch of San Francisco's ubiquitous baby tears ("birds need greens, too"), groundcovers are non-existent in this garden filled instead with varied and bright seasonal flower displays—no room in this inn for ground-hogging, flowerless covers. And the robins appreciate the bare, soggy earth at nest-building time.

Yet the tiny square garden doesn't feel hemmed in. The tall plants line the outside edges, while the center of the square is reserved for sunbathing and sun-loving flowers, reinforcing Telegraph Hill's reputation as one of the sunniest and warmest neighborhoods in San Francisco. Situated almost six miles from the Pacific Ocean and above the sheltered bay, the hill offers one of the finest city gardening environments on the Pacific Coast.

The hummingbirds—Rufous in the spring, Allen's in the spring and fall, and Anna's year 'round—are never without their favored single-flowering fuchsias; the double fuchsias are a bit complicated for these miniature machines on the fly. The fragile-looking hummingbirds head straight for the brilliant trumpet and jasmine vines covering the north property line; columbine, lobelia, impatiens, delphinium, nasturtium and pelargonium flowers—all quite easy and uncomplicated to grow in San Francisco—provide added nourishment.

Without the flowers and greens, of course, few insects would hover for birds to feed on. Only one pest in this garden escapes eradication by the birds: the annoying white fly that hides on the undersides of pelargoniums particularly. The birds won't attack, so the whiteflies receive periodic blasts from the garden hose as a substitute for the natural predators, who work so diligently to erase other troublesome bugs. Spiders don't last long, and even snails are snapped up by mockingbirds.

In addition to feeding on abundant nandina, juniper, and pyracantha seeds and berries in fall and winter, the birds obligingly plant seeds too. A rare—for San Francisco—Valley Oak (*Quercus lobata*) recently surfaced in her south flower border next to a mysterious seedling of the equally rare California Black Oak (*Quercus kelloggii*); they'll be allowed to stay until someone comes to claim them.

So in tune with nature and the natural cycles of her plants, this gardener has already allowed a seedling of her 20-year old Bailey's Acacia to take hold in the shadow of the parent tree, knowing that these spectacular January bloomers from Australia are short-lived and this one is due for retirement soon; the expected gap in her north border will fill in faster with the advance planning.

Surprisingly, birds of prey, including the sparrow hawk year-round and the sharp-shinned hawk in winter, are favorites too. These larger birds are allowed to do what they do best—thin abundant populations of field mice and the more common bird species, finches in particular.

Mrs. deLaet supplements the food supply with hulled sunflowers and wild bird seed. The feeders, placed just outside her studio window, give pleasure in winter when she can be closer to the birds. "I don't think the seeds attract the birds as much as the natural environment does," she insists. The "natural" environment of Grace deLaet's garden is not only far superior to the original landscape, it is a refuge on a flyway for winged visitors.

Downtown skyscraper looms above this Telegraph Hill garden, five blocks—as the crow flies—north of the Financial District.

—NORTH

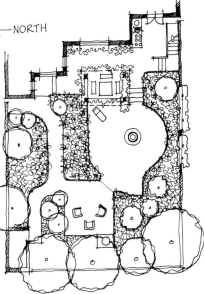

'Peace' and 'Chicago Peace' roses, which would stand out in any flower bed, simply blend in with all the other bright flowers Grace deLaet uses to attract birds to her garden.

The birds hover over these colorful flowers, seeking nectar and shelter.

*A
Tropical Garden
on Potrero Hill*

In cities worldwide, townhouses and apartment houses line the streets one after the other, with little distinction along the endless rows—until an innovative owner or tenant decides to make a splash. Where conformity rules, bold designs stay under wraps. Here is an owner who not only boldly redesigned his city home, he captured the essence of his make-over by surrounding the house with slender, graceful tropical plants. Had he simply redesigned the house, without adding the tropical surrounds, the effect would be only half as striking.

The starkness of the straight, pink-washed walls is softened by feathery foliage of palms and ferns, and enhanced by the giant leaves of banana, strelitzia and gunnera. As it is, the finished product produces great pleasure for passers-by; a fine gift to the street in a neighborhood that takes tropical designs with ease. The house and garden would be wildly out of place, for example, in a more traditional neighborhood, but Potrero Hill sits on the sunny side of San Francisco, open to views and new ideas.

Owner Larry Masnada enlisted the help of Padraig McCrory, and others, in the garden redesign. Admitting he'd rather live in Hawaii, the owner collected some of his own plants, then asked Mr. McCrory to track down unusual varieties not readily available in San Francisco nurseries. Mr. McCrory, experienced in southern California gardening design, found many rare plants, illustrating why a landscape designer's plant *sources* are as important as his plant identification skills.

Mr. McCrory then fitted the enormous specimens into a tight, 15 × 30 ft. street-side site, yet the overall effect seems spacious rather than crowded. He weaved wiring around new-found rocks to create the underpinnings for hillocks in the front, north facing garden, then installed the necessary mist system to keep the tree trunks and the ground covers moist. The light reflected off the bright walls is enough to keep the shade-lovers growing, before the winter winds wipe out advances and create the greatest threat to this transplanted landscape.

The rainless summer is, in fact, the peak season in Mr. McCrory's tropical garden—but not for the reasons generally associated with high summer in full flower. The tropical garden is fresh and green from its new spring growth and not yet cut down by damaging winds which cross Potrero Hill each afternoon. Color, in this tropical garden, is mostly green, with the most vibrant flowers placed around the sheltered pool in the back, protected, garden.

The afternoon summer wind, which announces the oncoming fog a mile or two to the west, rips through exposed plantings and eventually weakens the less hardy. Fortunately, the big house and high walls protect the back and side gardens, but the front has only the curved 8-ft. high staircase to protect the street garden from the advancing winds. Remembering that in natural tropical surroundings, these same plants thrive without the luxury of man-made wind-breaks, or high (pink-washed) garden walls, the battered city specimens soon recover, but look their best before the even more damaging winter storms arrive.

Orchids and orchid look-alikes provide the color accents, with careful selection of shade-tolerant terrestrial orchids for the front sunless garden. The orchid-like flower on the curious, prickly street tree of *Chorisia speciosa* deserves its common name, 'Los Angeles Beauty', indicating its pervasive presence near Hollywood High in southern California, where Mr. McCrory first found it.

A rare Alexandra Palm and its more common relative, the King Palm, vie for attention in the street garden, along with the enormous leaves of Elephant's Ear (*Colocasia esculenta*), which quickly fills in gaps below. A Bamboo Palm lives up to its name, and a giant Bird of Paradise (*Strelitzia nicolai*) sends up fans of banana-like leaves before the subtle (unlike its dazzling, common relative, *S. reginae's*) show of flowers. Even the "Inside-out-Flower" (*Vancouveria planipetala*) is chosen for its feathery ground-covering foliage rather than its tiny insignificant white flowers.

Like the turn-of-the-century San Francisco debut of the exotic *Victoria Regia*, many of these curious tropical plants in Mr. McCrory's garden are rare or one-of-a-kind today, waiting for popular—and, more importantly, nursery trade—acceptance. The current vogue for rare and exotic plants has, even in the past few years, produced a greater selection of more unusual species, although Mr. McCrory must still hunt in nurseries far afield for his tropical collection.

The hunt is as important as the catch, and is one reason for this garden's success. The garden, in turn, is the reason why the entire make-over dazzles rather than dulls the senses. In cities, where achievements are, of necessity, viewed close at hand, architectural and natural face-lifts, side by side, make striking combinations. Viewed together, the gift to the street seems even more stunning, and telegraphs a reminder that luxuriant greens can easily transport the city-weary to the tropics, if only for one brief, passing moment.

Palms and ferns cover the mounding groundcover to create a splendid tropical garden on Potrero Hill. (JSH photos)

View of the front garden from the entry stairway. The lush greens evoke teeming tropics, exactly as the owner intended.

Enormous leaves of *Gunnera chilensis* attract attention in this hilltop garden, shown with designer, Padraig McCrory.

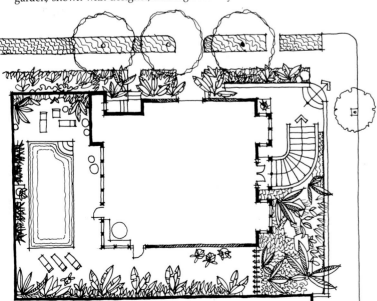

*An
Apple Orchard
on
Buena Vista Hill*

The earliest settlers, in any city, have the advantage of choosing the sunniest sites, with the best views, on soil (perhaps) rich and ready, for a town house and vegetable garden close in. In San Francisco, where the views come in superlatives, but the fog and sand dunes advance from the Pacific to the Bay, the sites chosen were, of necessity, on the eastern, sheltered side of the peninsula, or on the lee side of the city's hills.

The earliest residents of Buena Vista Hill had all the amenities save one: the distance from town was a long, three-mile journey to the then-remote hillside in the geographical center of the modern city. Even the remoteness had its advantages: more elbow room, and finer soil—a mixture of sand and clay.

The Buena Vista Orchard today thrives on a commanding hilltop site chosen early on for its location on the lee side of the hill. In this urban orchard, old apple varieties, unavailable commercially today, reclaim territory lost to the apple industry's mass-produced kinds—'Golden Delicious' and 'Red Delicious' sold everywhere. Advice was easy to come by for this gardener; predictably, each advisor had a different list of the best apples in the mild, frost-free city enclosure. So he set out to discover the best varieties by the oldest of testing methods: trial and error. Patience has paid off; the verdict is already in on many of the 33 varieties tested here in the past decade.

Each September, when the crop is ready for harvest, the owner of this experimental orchard sheds the poor performers and keeps the best varieties for further observation. Only a dozen apple varieties will remain after the current crop is pared down in the next few years. 'Winter Banana', for example, an apple enthusiastically grown in warm coastal climates, performs poorly in this garden, blooming at the wrong time of year and showing other tell-tale signs of stress. Out it goes, along with 'Sierra Beauty' whose name (along with its growing requirements) suggests mountain, rather than city, surrounds.

The successes, however, far outnumber the failures. One particular favorite in Great Britain—planted by the acre in the Kent countryside, and affectionately labeled "the finest of all apples" by Pacific Horticulture editor George Waters—'Cox's Orange Pippin' performs exceedingly well on Buena Vista Hill, and will be nurtured for years to come in this city garden. Another success, for numbers of apples produced, comes from an early American variety, 'Roxbury Russet', although the taste doesn't measure up to either the 'Cox's Orange Pippin' or the ubiquitous 'McIntosh', a good performer in San Francisco.

Thomas Jefferson's favorite apple, 'Esopus Spitzenburg', is on trial here, as is another apple discovered by Mr. Jefferson while Ambassador to France, the famous French winter apple, 'Calville Blanc d'Hiver'. The French apple is said to contain more vitamin C than an orange, and its elongated shape distinguishes it from other varieties in the orchard. The history of each apple makes the collecting all the more interesting for this gardener.

The reason why all these apples exist side by side without crowding one another is because each specimen is espaliered (derived from the Italian word 'spalla' for shoulder), closely trained against a trellis running the length of the garden. The walls of open latticework on the street allow for air circulation and neighborly visits, while providing a backbone for the trees; triple duty in a crowded city garden made more spacious with this ancient training technique.

Admittedly unscientific, the San Francisco apple observations follow years of research and farming for this gardener, also near the sea, in Nova Scotia. The farming instincts transport easily from coast to coast, but the diesel engine fumes and other city hazards come with the new territory. When the apple choices finally materialize from the Buena Vista Orchard, hundreds of city gardeners will benefit from this amateur's research on historic apples suited to the San Francisco climate.

Like Thomas Jefferson in his Monticello orchard long ago, this modern gardener will soon list his favorites, then pass along the observations, picking up converts, and delicious apples, along the way.

The sunny hilltop garden needs coldframe protection for tender herbs to get a good start. Basil now performs well with the added protection.

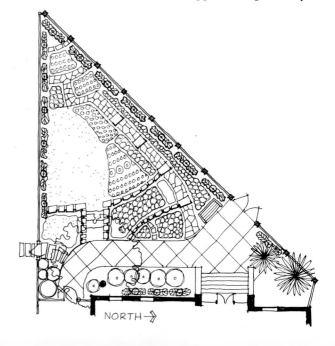

NORTH →

Stepping stones lead past vegetables, left, and children's flowers, right. Young espaliered apples lined against the trellis await their trials before permanent planting.

Bicycles parked under young espaliered apple, set in special container.

To save space in this small city garden, every bit of wall area, including the lattice boundary, is used, in this case, to support espaliered apples.

A SEPTEMBER GARDEN

A Rich Harvest in Noe Valley

An architect and an artist have shared this Noe Valley garden for 25 years, and the harvest improves with each passing year. The architect, Al Lanier, presides over the fall feast and dreams of the day he'll retire here, to his city garden that consumes entire weekends now. His wife, sculptress Ruth Asawa, spreads out her artwork in the garden's center, implants her sculptured masks like lichen in the garden walls, and paints the fresh flowers her husband brings in to her on weekend mornings.

The garden, unlike the detailed buildings and fine sculptures created during the week, is never finished, is always in need of another flower or another crop, is dirt just waiting for creative hands to touch. This garden is one of the most lived in, worked over, tilled and re-tilled piles of earth two city dwellers could hope to create, and the end is not yet in sight. That's the delight. "We're not happy until we have three plants in the space one should occupy; we also aren't happy until we move a plant four times!" says Mr. Lanier.

The boundaries, like the flowers, have moved, too, in the past 25 years. Eyeing a derelict patch nearby, down went the fence to make way for the easement purchased across adjoining property. "I decided if you could buy an easement for a driveway or a sewer, then you could buy an easement for a garden!" Mr. Lanier says. Another house, to the south, is a part of the moveable feast, too, with its vegetable and herb beds behind. Neighbors pitch in at planting time, then help to reap the rewards at harvest time. The more the flowers, the more the need for the shredder and chopper which moves too as flower beds intrude on its territory. From the spent stalks, broken branches and seed capsules, the shredder churns out fine mulch waiting for recycling into the earth below. The chopper filters out few undesireables, so the borage, morning glory and nasturtiums reappear year after year, invited or not, to brighten the beds. Even the encroaching black bamboo hedge ("It's my one Oriental plant") is recycled; the cut stems reappear as flower stakes.

The constant rearranging pays off for some, if not all, the thriving plants in this garden. The fall blooming Mexican Sunflower (*Tithonia rotundifolia*) now produces masses of daisy-like flowers which never appeared in its previous site; the bounty comes when the fuzzy seed balls are taken indoors for table arrangement.

Another novelty, the Tree Dahlia (*Dahlia imperialis*), reigns over the flower bed in the fall, reaching great heights until cut down by the winds from the west. It too must move, Mr. Lanier promises.

In the neat rows of raised vegetable beds, oregeno, winter savory and tarragon share space with lettuce (harvested one leaf at a time) and tomatoes. The apple, lemon and spearmints are confined to wooden bins, but the comfrey just keeps coming. Ruth Asawa's pickled plums, taken from her Japanese plum trees, are preserved and prized each year, as are other recipes from this chef's garden. And one specimen of a "chokeless choke" artichoke, a most reliable northern California coastal crop, is allowed in the flower bed for its ornamental value.

The artistic front entry garden only hints at the harvest beyond. Within dozens of niches in the brick walls, sculpted children's faces appear alongside other family members' masks. The grandchildren will soon occupy their places in another planned boundary wall. The intricate cobble wall design and walk design was a joint-effort, but the cobbles themselves were already sculpted by the sea when Ruth Asawa discovered them in a rubble heap at China Beach, on the city's northwest shoreline.

Gardening here, in the smallest of city patches, is a pleasure rather than a chore, and the signs of contentment (rather than containment) are in every border, in every corner. Guests come and go, and the garden always sends up a fresh, earthy scent for visitors and family members alike. The art of garden making has reached its perfection in this San Francisco garden, and the tools of this trade are not just pen, pencil and paintbrush, but time, trowel and spade.

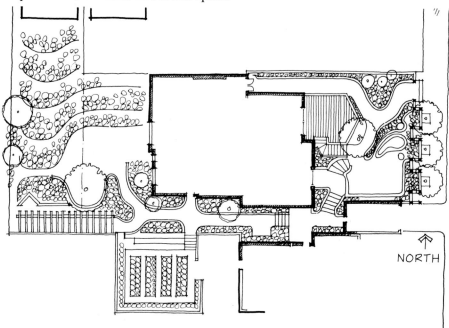

NORTH

Sculptress Ruth Asawa plants her artwork in the garden walls. Family members' masks line entry garden wall.

Vegetable beds produce abundant crops in this productive city garden.

The shredder grinds out a constant supply of seed and weeds and compost for this beautiful garden in Noe Valley. Lettuce and tomatoes grow in recessed garden beside the ornamental plants.

Grape arbor supports Concord Grape vine, while nasturtiums reseed themselves, below.

117

AN
OCTOBER
GARDEN

*A Formal
French Garden
Near Alta Plaza*

For the world traveler or weekend gardener only, here is a superb example of a 'borrowed' garden taken not from the textbooks but taken, instead, from perhaps the world's richest source of inspiration: Versailles and nearby formal French gardens. This miniature—25-ft. wide by 125-ft. long—French copy is formal, yet casually so. The bedding behind the borders is permanent rather than seasonal and needs very little attention, yet the garden is the center of attention every weekend when this busy couple settles in to their garden retreat.

The garden was only a "yard" 20 years ago when the 19th Century wood-frame house came on the market. Like budgets of newlyweds everywhere, little money remained for the garden make-over after the old house received a face lift. But here lies the ingenuity behind the formal French copy, and a lesson Louis XIV never learned: very little money went into this grand garden design and planting scheme. Rather, this couple relied on their intuitive fine taste, local plant sales, and particularly on city work crews with their clippings and cast-offs.

The four London Plane trees, for example, came from street prunings in front of their new home. With an eye for a bargain and another eye on their shade-less back yard, the owners struck cuttings from four left-over sycamore limbs, then perfectly placed their four new trees diagonally opposite one another, anchoring the far corners of the two long narrow green beds in the center of their back yard. More cuttings followed after the initial success, so the sycamore trees now form the essential formal backbone upon which the other plants play.

Tall, narrow hedging—to draw the eye outward and give the illusion of spaciousness—camouflages property lines on either side of the 25-ft. wide plot. Reliable hedging material of 8-ft. high pittosporum stands behind the Japanese boxwood edging which curves around the u-shaped concrete walkway. The Japanese boxwood, which needs three prunings a year, is an admitted mistake, a false economy at the time. The more expensive, but less rambunctious, English boxwood would be the edging choice today.

Around the perimeter of the property, airy latticework (copied from the deYoung Museum cafe in Golden Gate Park) marks the borders without creating a tunnel-like, closed-in effect. Latticework also allows more dappled sunlight in, a necessity in the cool San Francisco summers.

In winter, the plane trees lose their leaves, exposing the square beds of calla lilies edged with boxwood to warmth and light. More light also filters down to the centered cafe table and chairs where the antique dealer and his fashion executive wife spend warm winter weekends reading the newspaper, catching up on paperwork, and dreaming of their next trip to France. The owners reserve only three weekends a year for garden maintenance; the garden must hold its own against summer winds, against weeks of neglect, against encroaching Texas root rot from the neighboring yard.

Low maintenance gardens conjure up images of forlorn juniper and ivy struggling on their own while garden owners head for the golf course or fishing stream—any outdoor diversion but the garden and its attendant "chores". In this case, however, low maintenance does not mean low esteem or familiarity with other low maintenance city gardens. The garden is cared for in the best way this couple knows how: by eagerly translating design ideas from abroad, and, once home, by relaxing and absorbing their handsome design on warm San Francisco days. The price tag: next to nothing; the rewards: fit for a king.

The plane trees, rooted from street tree cuttings, now frame the garden beds.

118

The long, narrow garden, seen from the back stairway landing.

Looking back toward the house, tall Calla Lily leaves remain green while the trees turn color. Laurel hedges, right, above low Japanese boxwood. Pittosporum hedge, left.

119

A Miniature Japanese Garden in Laurel Heights

The Golden Gate Bridge is San Francisco's most celebrated vista. In city gardens on Telegraph and Russian Hill, in Presidio and Pacific Heights, sunrises and sunsets over the magnificent structure are taken for granted. San Francisco gardeners on neighboring hillsides catch glimpses of the red towers or listen to the moaning of the fog horns which signal the bay beyond. The bridge is the backdrop that steals the show, that orients the visitor, that brings man and nature together in a most pleasing design.

This hemmed-in Laurel Hill garden is more like city gardens everywhere; it has no vista, no distant fog horns, no landscape to 'borrow.' Three-story townhouses are packed in and peer down on one another, with little privacy or sense of the natural wonders beyond. The challenge was to bring nature to the back door, to camouflage the intrusions, to create a miniature, soothing world in this squared, 30 ft. enclosure.

Oriental cultures do this best—recreate the mysterious moods of nature in uncompromising tight spaces; the more difficult the site, the more inspiration is summoned. Both the Chinese and Japanese have influenced this city's design: the Chinese for their bold architectural treatments, and the Japanese for their subtle, soft, subdued garden designs. The Chinese occupy a more distinct presence, but it is the Japanese who have most influenced garden design here, who have shared their cultural heritage in their adopted city. The natural elements that played such an important part in their island setting across the Pacific are here, too, for the asking, on the hills and in the valleys by the Golden Gate.

To study Japanese garden design from textbooks is to grasp a partial essence before attempting an Americanized version of Oriental design. To prevail upon a first or second-generation native son to impart the Japanese style is an honor that San Franciscans take, like the Golden Gate Bridge sunsets, for granted. The owners of this Laurel Hill garden—she is a flower arranger, his hobby is greenhouse gardening—called in their friend, Ittsei Nakagawa, a Hiroshima survivor, to transform this site.

This was no ordinary garden advisor—Mr. Nakagawa only transforms gardens for friends, and only on weekends. During the week, Mr. Nakagawa works in his pin-striped suit, in a highrise downtown. On weekends, he designs and builds Japanese landscapes, and selects clients as carefully as each rock in each garden. The client must promise to maintain the artful arrangement; in turn, Mr. Nakagawa presents a 'before' and 'after' photograph album as a keepsake of the makeover.

The renovation, in this case, occupied 30 weekend days spanning four months. Viewing the finished product is to be transformed into the wilderness where rushing water soothes the spirit, where rocks are sculped by time, where time seems eternal. The time warp is even more astonishing given the realization that this 'finished' landscape is exactly as it was three years ago, the day it was completed. Thus two cultures merged to blend the American need for instant success with the Japanese talent for timeless tradition.

Around the perimeter of the property, a handsome wooden fence, of a light, classic Japanese design, quietly encloses the space and sets the mood. For ease of maintenance and flower gathering, a pebbled pathway encircles the space but is hidden by shrubbery and the majestic waterfall. For the waterfall and bridge, each rock was individually selected for signs of grace and age. "No two rocks are alike," says Mr. Nakagawa. "No two persons are alike, no two plants are alike. Each rock has a shape and character and must be individually chosen." Every stone was set against the next, then wedges placed beneath the mass, to precisely imitate a natural waterfall. "If you go to the mountains, there are millions of rocks out there, unnoticed," Mr. Nakagawa observes. While rocks in Chinese gardens are individual specimens in themselves, stonework in a Japanese composition is subservient to the entire picture.

But in the cities, civilization intrudes on even the most carefully created fantasies. The day the waterfall began to flow, the neighbors' complaints of noise also began to flow. An ingenious solution resulted. Mr. Nakagawa readjusted the cascade by rearranging the rocks, before toying with the hidden pump to soften the sound of the falling water. The pump still moves 50 gallons a minute, but the altered stonework reduced the sound.

For all the design elements employed, the plants still predominate, as traditional Japanese garden-making has dictated for centuries. The bonsai specimens existed on the site but are now woven into the composition. The smaller plants are centered; the larger plantings seem to mysteriously emerge from behind the stones and shrubs. To simply choose, sight unseen, a "five-gallon" plant, without inspecting its every angle, is unthinkable not only for Mr. Nakagawa but all Japanese garden-makers.

The southwest-facing greenhouse is unlike any other. Designed by Mr. Nakagawa as a subtle—rather than, as in Chinese gardens, a bold architectural—transition between the starkness of the house and the soft, sculpted landscape, the enclosure grew smaller as the garden plans grew grander. But tomatoes know no bounds and thrive in the cool enclosure.

Just outside the greenhouse, the seasons change while the water washes against the rocks. The sea breezes dictate the shape while centuries of garden tradition successfully cross the Pacific.

Surrounding townhouses close in on this small city garden but the masterful miniature landscape evokes the distant countryside.

The greenhouse makes a smooth transition from the stark townhouse to the soft landscape.

NORTH

Each rock was carefully selected and set in place to control the flow and set the final scene.

*A Vast
Japanese
Landscape
Overlooking
Lobos Creek*

The setting for a city garden couldn't be better: a natural creek wandering below, fog horns brooding beyond, and a vast preserved landscape just outside the garden walls. But 20 years ago a high wooden fence, held back the distant landscape, and inside the walls, a cold concrete walkway encircled a square, boring patch of lawn. Around the perimeter of the property, rows of regimented modern roses, overgrown and thorny, were incompatible with hide-and-seek plans of four small children. Utility and ease of maintenance existed on site; beauty, on the other hand, was clearly missing.

This Richmond District garden, less than a mile from the sea, clearly needed rejuvenation. An offer of help came from quite an unexpected source—their Japanese gardener, Eddy Harada, who had never before and has only twice since designed a San Francisco garden. He spoke little English then, but went straight to his task, moving and, creating mountains, building bridges, sculpting trees, raising, then lowering, waterworks.

His exquisite landscape transcends cultural barriers and makes an eloquent case for tradition as the best tutor. The inherent Japanese ability to turn the ordinary into the magical, and then have it stand the test of time, is played out here, even after years of hard play by four healthy children.

As the transformation unfolded, the owners watched in amazement as a miniature landscape took shape in the hands of their Japanese designer. Viewing his waterfall from different vantage points, Mr. Harada would proceed only when satisfied that his cascade fell perfectly, as it might in the wilderness. After months of lifting and rolling boulders, his attention to the smallest details paid off handsomely.

A tiny stone bridge, which, with beginners bad luck, collapsed on its first go-round, spans a dry creek bed. A wisteria-laden arbor hides the fish pond beyond, and rounded river pebbles replace the cold concrete paths. In the center of the remaining lawn, a bonsai of Black Pine stands on its own, a stark symbol of nature at its most inspiring.

The lawn is lush now while the backdrop of hawthorn, crabapple and maple trees adds a forested feeling where scruffy rose bushes once competed for attention. Away from the house, the lawn edging is curved, rather than squared, and mysteriously disappears under streambeds and stones.

Most of these trees drop their leaves in autumn, allowing winter light to reach the floor below. The composition is soothing, as is the autumn color—subtle rather than strident. The red berries of cotoneaster and hawthorn, the rust and orange leaf colors on Japanese maples add to the overall effect. No individual plant stands out, yet each plant is essential in setting the mood.

For children, the miniature landscape fuels the imagination during transitions from forest to glen, from waterfall to streambed. For older observers, Mr. Harada's landscape is a moment in time, in contrast to rapidly changing time just beyond the garden gate. Few town dwellers could ask for more—a classic garden retreat from the pressures all around.

The lifting and hauling has taken its toll of Mr. Harada. Semi-retired, he manages a thriving bonsai trade, aptly named "Eddy's Bonsai," near the Stow Lake entrance to Golden Gate Park. His world continues in miniature, only now, even more so.

A tall wooden fence held back the creek-side view and beds of prickly roses edged the concrete walkway around the square patch of lawn.

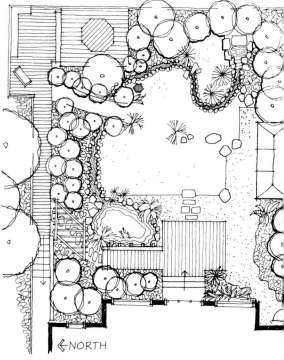

←NORTH

122

The garden today, with the same orientation, looking northeast, but with a waist-high, open fence. The interior space, transformed by Japanese gardener Eddy Harada into a miniature landscape.

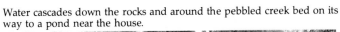

Maple and wisteria turn color, then lose their leaves in autumn, opening up the arbor in winter.

Water cascades down the rocks and around the pebbled creek bed on its way to a pond near the house.

Tool shed masquerading as a tea house. Abelia in autumn bloom, foreground.

*A
Highrise
Balcony Garden
on Russian Hill*

City skyscrapers offer little opportunity for communion with nature; the higher above the ground, the fiercer the gardening challenge. Some urbanites are content with reliable but soon dusty indoor plants: parlor palms in dark corners, shriveled pelargoniums in sunny windows. Others, fortunate enough to have an open-air balcony all too frequently line up cast-off indoor plants behind outdoor plants which a nurseryman promised as wind-resistant but which soon take on the appearance of primroses in the arctic regions. Permanent water stains mark the spots where plastic and clay pots once camped out in the cold—a dreary environment indeed, for people and plants.

How, then, to turn these lifeless environments into gardens in the clouds? These two 18th floor balconies, separated by a glassed-in enclosure, offer two wildly different solutions to the challenge without shouting about the fine finished result.

Both balconies face north and are therefore in shade most of the year. Both are in the direct path of San Francisco's westerly winds yet receive little winter rain because of the overhang above. The one great advantage, which for gardenmaker Stephen Marcus actually turned into a slight design drawback: a smashing view of the Golden Gate Bridge to the west (or left) of both balconies.

Mr. Marcus contended with two different assignments for the two balconies: the westerly 18 ft. should be an extension of the living room with its Oriental artifacts, yet not detract from the Golden Gate view beyond. The easterly 18 ft. balcony, off the bedroom, could be more frivolous and flowery, and seasonally changeable. Separated by the protected enclosure, each balcony creates a different mood, yet each, in its own way, softly bridges the visual barrier between the stark, man-made, concrete deckings close at hand, and the distant Golden Gate.

The westerly balcony is the contemplative compartment, set off to the side in order to enhance the direct Golden Gate view less than three miles away. The traditional Japanese sleeve gate was the only artifact on hand, but needed to be weaved into the ultimate design. The wooden gate is placed on an angle not only to baffle the westerly wind, but to add a sense of distance and space, particularly effective with the ferns and greenery placed between the gate and the concrete wall beyond.

With a working space only 3½ ft. wide, one strategically placed chrysanthemum bowl holds a reflecting pool and balances the outer side of the composition, while a taller antique vase visually anchors the gate nearer the windows simultaneously camouflaging the curled-up water hose inside its frame. Both carefully-chosen vases are softened further by surrounding greens—the pool is enclosed by a single cedar bonsai whose artfully pruned branches are reflected in the rippling water.

The center of the western-most, mood-evoking garden is not only left open and free of marching clay pots, all the concrete underpinnings are hidden from view by a cleverly-designed wooden platform that elevates the plane a foot or two above the original floor. The wooden platform—which has built-in recesses for submerging the wooden pots full of earth and greens—is covered with an inch of sharp 'birds-eye' gravel. The final touch, the tie-in that makes the contemplative scene work, is the stepping stones, placed in the traditional 1-3-1 Oriental order, linking the meditation bench on the right with the bamboo gate, pool and greens on the left.

The walls of the 'gaggle-of-bunny balcony', as Mr. Marcus affectionately calls the eastern-most terrace, were washed to blend in with the San Francisco sky, and its floors covered with tiles. Two antique pots—one tall, the other smaller and rounded—precisely reflect the shape and size of the two on the western balcony. The smaller container holds a dwarf Pittosporum—that sturdy, wind-resistant native of the Pacific Rim—clipped only twice a year. Nearby, at the foot of the sliding glass doors, is the seasonal flower display. This eastern balcony, were it not for its link to its western neighbor, is more typical of balcony gardens everywhere in its simplicity.

At sunset, however, when the pale light begins to fade off the bay and the soft light at the writing desk takes over, the two balconies merge as one moody bridge between the sky and the glass enclosure. This is the time of day when nature rests, but here, on the 18th floor, engulfed by two outdoor scenes, nature is closer than for some house dwellers below.

Mood is one element; reality is another—how is all of this kept lush and green and how are those pebbles restrained from clogging the water drain? Hand watering, a formidable chore even for San Franciscans on the sandy soil below, soon proved overwhelming on this balcony 200 ft. above the sea. A battery-operated timed watering system is now installed, adding another man-made element to the overall effort and effect. The built-in wooden platform keeps the pebbles above the filter, while a trap door allows for routine cleaning.

These Russian Hill balconies remind the city dweller that man-made bridges can indeed be as appealing as natural bridges, if nature is, in the process, understood and understated. The reflection of the cedar branch in the water of the chrysanthemum bowl, which itself recalls the bay waters below, is a subtle and soothing recollection of nature beyond. The placement, off center, of the dominant terrace garden in order to highlight the magnificent Golden Gate Bridge view beyond, is to understand just who is the star and who is the understudy in San Francisco's grand scheme. And one long narrow terrace, divided in two by a glass enclosure, evokes or envelopes, depending on its creator.

Stepping stones lead to traditional gate and chrysanthemum bowl in the western-most balcony garden. Wooden planking underneath the pebbles hides handiwork while raising floor area to meet sliding glass doors.

The greens seem closer as the day draws to an end outside this 18th floor balcony on Russian Hill.

The east balcony, set on tiled floor, holds potted pittosporum and seasonal flowers. Golden Gate Bridge appears on western horizon.

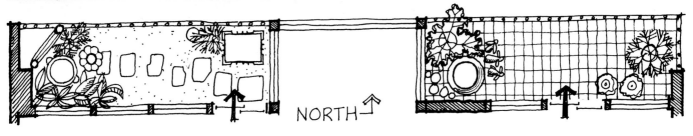

NORTH ⇧

*A
Boxwood
Garden
on a Rooftop
in Presidio
Heights*

In skyscraper-dominated cities, and in cities like San Francisco where vistas unfold far below hilltop houses, rooftops often cover the landscape, substituting for, and masquerading as, earth and soil below. The hard edges seem to reinforce harsh city surroundings. Yet viewed from highrises and hilltops, one highly visible rooftop, transformed, becomes not only an elevated pleasure-ground for its owner (or cooperative owners), but a pleasure, too, for nearby neighbors.

If, as in this case, the garage rooftop covers the width of the property and its imposing presence constitutes the main view from every back window, transformation is inevitable. Mr. and Mrs. Edmund B. MacDonald, owners of this Presidio Heights mansion, with its big old garage to match, sought the help of architect George Livermore 25 years ago in masking the intrusion on their back lot.

The starkness and steepness of the back garden was matched by the stiffness of the tiny squared-off patch of front yard lawn wedged between the sidewalk and the house, offering little privacy or outdoor retreat, and actually making the imposing house seem even more so. The lines needed softening, the two distinct areas—shaded and windy in back, and sunny yet exposed in front—needed vastly different solutions.

Mr. Livermore, as adept at transforming gardens as architectural details, set out a series of boxwood enclosures on the garage roof, with paths of tiny pebbles around the hedges, and evergreen ground-covers within the enclosures. The handsome and eye-catching design, when seen from above by the owners and surrounding neighbors, invites a stroll through its green geometric patterns.

The touch of green also brings closer the sweep of cypress treetops from the Presidio military enclave separating Presidio Heights from the Golden Gate Bridge. The tips of the bridge towers are visible on clear days and create a stunning backdrop for this sophisticated, easy care garden.

The wind off the Bay makes this north-facing garden less than ideal for most plants and people; simple, easy greens—dwarf creeping fig, Japanese boxwood, privet and juniper—provide the interest, and assure the owners of easy maintenance, as they requested years ago.

The south-facing front garden, while almost as confining a space as the garage roof, serves quite a different purpose—while the rooftop is admired from afar, the sun-drenched front garden is well-used and gardened. Two tricks of the trade were employed by George Livermore to transform the sunny but tiny front yard: He planted an airy hedge of pittosporum at the street line, then excavated the lawn area to create a sunken sun trap, covered in warming tiles, and edged with raised planting beds, filled with colorful flowers year-round.

The dazzling flower displays, designed by Hilary Gordon, bring the changing San Francisco seasons close to the MacDonald front door, while the cool greens in the back garden remain on view year-round, exactly as planned 25 years ago. "There was no place to get outside before; it was a most negative aspect of this house," recalls Mrs. MacDonald. "But when the garden came into being, the house really seemed to have everything."

Mr. Livermore, whose family, for generations, has contributed to California conservation efforts (Mt. Livermore on Angel Island in San Francisco Bay is but one reminder), takes as much pride in these two small gardens as he does in his grandest architectural achievements. His garden designs—and his shaping of this city's landscape—are evident throughout the northern slopes of San Francisco.

In a city where space is at a premium, and houses often cover entire lot lines, the greening of a rooftop and the creation of a small, sunken, sun trap might seem minor compared to sweeping makeovers on country estates. Yet Mr. Livermore's handsome gardens are a civilized approach to a stark city reality, and highlight the greater gardening challenge: transforming tiny leftover space into magic gardens.

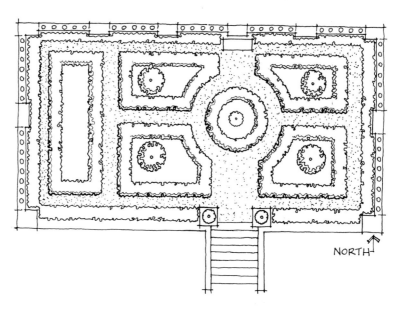

NORTH

Seen from the house, looking north, formal design holds shape year-round. Golden Gate Bridge towers in the distance, left.

Close up of pebbles, boxwood and privet accents in this mostly maintenance-free, windy, roof garden. The garden is little used but often viewed.

The sunny front garden, hollowed out and tiled over to trap the sun and heat. Flowers fill the raised beds, and change with the seasons. This small space is well used.

127

A Fern Allee on a Roofdeck on Telegraph Hill

With the emergence of the environmental movement 25 years ago, city squares, parks and gardens took on a decidedly country air as landscape architects struggled to interpret modern mores. Like the '60s, these country lanes, squiggly paths and overgrown plantings are fading from view. Formal gardens, straight lines, austere plantings, are making a comeback in the city, in the view of globe-trotting architect and artist Barbara Stauffacher-Solomon.

Just a few years ago, her 10 × 10-ft. Telegraph Hill roofdeck was a mountain habitat transplanted to the city, a tower of trees reaching for the sky against dark redwood paneling which lined the outside walls. The roots below were reaching, too—for the bedroom, living room and kitchen located directly beneath the roofdeck. When the rains came, the roots reached further, bringing the soggy mass into the townhouse below.

Only the simplest formal design would erase the existing "romantic wilderness" that spilled everywhere in this compact garden eight years ago. The tall trees were yanked from the sidelines, the redwood walls whitewashed, and the whole compartment redesigned to complement the tiny townhouse overlooking the northern waterfront.

The restrained solution is simple, straightforward, and fresh. Eight giant ferns, in matching pots, surround the tiny cafe table, forming the letter "T" in their arrangement. Four ferns, placed two on either side, lead the eye up an allee from the back door to the table and chairs; the four remaining ferns form a backdrop behind the table. "I'm a great formalist; this is my ordered arrangement."

She acknowledges that formal gardens have been out of fashion for many years. "If you put trees in a straight line you were evil!" Romantic wildernesses, she insists, have no place in cities: "To try to turn a small city garden into the Sierras I think is madness."

For her arrangement, she went to the store where many San Franciscans buy their indoor plants—Cost Plus, 10 minutes from her house near the foot Telegraph Hill—and, with no preconceptions, picked out eight of the largest ferns in stock. When the plants lined up in perfect position, on her roofdeck, she settled on that design, and hasn't moved the arrangement since. "I never touch it; once it's there, it's there."

She won't add color, so the yearly expense of perking up the garden is non-existent here. On color in the garden, Mrs. Stauffacher-Solomon admits: "I like the gardens of Italy in winter when they're not mucked up with lots of little red geraniums that the Italians feel they have to do for the tourists . . . I like the gardens of Europe when they're green."

Rooftops are as important for outdoor retreats as their grounded counterparts are, at street level; to have an accessible rooftop, and ignore its potential living space is unthinkable to Mrs. Stauffacher-Solomon: "If you have a small apartment in the city, I think it's very important that you have someplace to go outside. Otherwise, the view is just wallpaper."

Here is a garden whose owner has strong views on design, and on cities as visually exciting places to live. The smallest rooftop, the largest plaza, are each spaces waiting for an imprint. In her opinion, Alta Plaza, Union Square, and particularly, the Marina Green, are the city's handsomest, most beautifully designed parks; a roof or patio could vie for best garden, with the same principles employed in the pretty parks: lean, ordered plantings, directness of pathways, and simple, restrained plan.

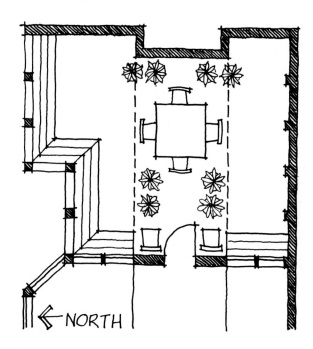

NORTH

Without overhanging trees, the trellis now filters sun, creates shadow interest on the potted ferns. Golden Gate Bridge and bay in distant view, over Telegraph Hill rooftops.

Potted ferns surround cafe table and chairs, setting the scene. View from back door, connected to main living area by interior bridge.

An Orchestrated
Green Garden
on
Buena Vista Hill

One of the finest hedges in the city—a massive and meticulous Coastal Tea, *Leptospermum laevigatum*—frames the entry to this Queen Anne home and reveals the owner's plan to orchestrate her greens for year-round effect. She admits she's not a gardener but an architect and planner; she insists that "the garden should be planned with the house, my dear, with the house." Rarely does a flower appear in this serene garden, and only then from pink or white buds above shiny, green leaves on camellias in winter.

The effect Mrs. Paul Page Austin has achieved after 32 years in her Buena Vista hilltop garden is startling in its attention to detail. The hedging across the deeply recessed back garden is carefully crafted so, when viewed from the upstairs sitting room, the hedge tops will "touch" the bay waterline on the horizon three miles to the east. The hedges on either side of the back garden "step" down the hillside to conceal neighboring houses while allowing as much light as possible into this east-facing garden.

It is no accident that the garden and house fit together so well. Three decades ago, friends urged her to try an Oriental design—"all the rage in those days"—but she resisted, having just returned from England. A bold design of gazebo, ivy oval and backdrop of surrounding greenery jumps up at the viewer three floors above the garden while the suggested miniature Oriental landscape would have receded into the lower level, she points out. She needed help at the start and knew she had the right man when German designer Herman Hein—who shaped many Marin County gardens in the 1940s and '50s after the Golden Gate Bridge opened a northern passage from the city—showed up in his lederhosen to take charge of the original design.

After months of searching for the perfect columns from a proper demolished mansion, Mrs. Austin handed them to Mr. Hein who then dramatically placed the columns off-center, in the far corner of the garden. "Most designers would have put that gazebo right in the middle of the back; he put it in the corner and made everything turn around toward it! Everything curves toward the gazebo," she exclaims. That trick, in her opinion, "enlarged the property and made it more interesting."

The ivy oval is surrounded by a carefully constructed gravel bed. "Most people just throw the gravel out—that's no good at all!" Days before the gravel went in, the soil was tamped down so it was absolutely flat and then it was watered lightly. A very thin layer of cement was thrown on the wet ground, and it "hardened just enough so that it holds the gravel where it should be, and the gravel doesn't go down into the ground."

Each limb on every specimen receives equal attention; nothing is allowed to outgrow its allotted space. The 15 ft. New Zealand (or Coastal) Tea Tree (*Leptospermum laevagatum*) hedge in the front entryway needs constant trimming, but the resulting dense evergreen screen rewards its owner by filtering out dust and noise from the adjoining city street. The front hedge has a hidden backbone of solid iron cross-piping to keep the greenery upright when the wind blows in from the sea.

Nearby in the front entry, Mattress Vine (*Muehlenbeckia complexa*) needs almost as much attention. In fact, only an extremely confident San Francisco gardener—a category into which this owner falls—would tolerate, let alone plant, this tiny beguiling mattress vine which slowly but surely engulfs nearby neighbors in a favorable maritime climate.

The back garden hedges of eugenia, Monterey Cypress and pittosporum need two or three clippings a year. The back garden trees—a magnificent Redwood (*Sequoia sempervirens*) towering above the southeast wing, a fine Silver Dollar Gum (*Eucalyptus polyanthemos*) weeping its branches near the gazebo, and a Silver Birch (*Betula pendula*) turning golden in late autumn along the north boundary—are pruned yearly by a tree surgeon. The Silver Birch branches perform double duty, first for landscaping needs and once cut, as supple weavings in homemade baskets.

She purposely chose rambunctious, fast-growing eucalyptus, eugenia and cypress because those plants spring back so quickly after repeated trimming; slower growers take months to recover, leaving a tell-tale gap in her small city garden where every inch is always on view.

The absence of flowers in this green garden is no accident, though the owner is a noted flower arranger and long-time member of the San Francisco Garden Club. Ivy is the green most often used in her flower arrangements, and the variegated varieties are her particular favorites. The handsome scarlet and green eugenia leaves are favorites too for her floral creations. "Flowers are beautiful but when they get shabby. . . . . what do you do?" she asks. "Gardens that always have that residue of half broken down plants and flowers . . . I knew that wasn't for me." And yet, she spends as much, if not more, time in her garden than many "dirt" gardeners, collecting, clipping, sweeping, and thinking . . . about the next textured leaf for tomorrow's exquisite floral arrangement.

Endnote: During production of this book, Mrs. Austin, eighty-eight years old, moved across the street to a spacious apartment where she now orchestrates the greens for dozens of residents, and relishes her new assignment. Her old Buena Vista hilltop garden is safely in the hands of Mr. Anthony Zanze, who purchased the house "for the garden!" and—for continuity and a happy ending—employs the same gardener and tree trimmers to orchestrate those greens.

Herman Hein placed the columns off to one side rather than in the center of the back garden. The ivy oval faces the corner gazebo.

Looking uphill from the gazebo, the ivy and evergreens frame the Silver Birch, clinging to its color into December.

The back garden, recessed two stories below the living quarters. The bold design, in Mrs. Austin's view, brings the sunken garden closer to the upper level. Ivy oval off center, faces gazebo.

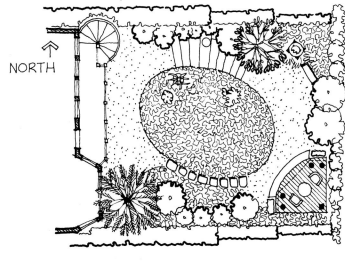

NORTH

The manicured hedge is backed by heavy iron pipes to protect the tall growth from San Francisco winds.

Special thanks to the Golden Gate Park gardeners, pictured here, who gave so freely of their time to make this book a garden book, rather than a guide book. Their knowledge of, and enthusiasm for, their craft, is an inspiration for all who garden in this seaside city. (Photo by Henry Bowles)

Special thanks too, to the editors of *Sunset* books, for producing, years ago, *The Sunset Western Garden Book*—affectionately called *The (Green) Bible* by West Coast gardeners. With that valuable reference in hand, San Francisco Zone 17 gardeners, in particular, leap right past the first "Will that flower in the fog?" phase onto more creative plateaus, all the while clinging to their A-Z *Sunset* guide.

INDEX

Mattress, or wire, vine (*Muehlenbeckia complexa*) makes a handsome clipped hedge against this San Francisco garden gate. The evergreen vine, originally imported from New Zealand, is seen in many old San Francisco gardens, rambling over everything in its path if left unchecked. (JSH photograph)

133